Ann love

so much

with

Bryan

Mr. Nease gratefully acknowledges photographs courtesy of James Whittaker, Jake Jackobson, Robert Ragsdale, Ken Duncan and Michael Ortiz

ISBN:
1-4196-5529-9
ISBN-13:
9781419655296

Visit www.booksurge.com to order additional copies.

Byron Nease

BEHIND THE MASK... No More

A Phantom Stars' Journey
Through Love, Abuse, Fame,
Loss to Re-Invention

ABOUT BYRON NEASE AND
BEHIND THE MASK... No More

"An open, enlightening and inspirational debut book by Byron Nease. He has willingly shared with readers what many of us fear to share with our closest friends and family. His story will make you laugh and cry but, most importantly, it will fill you with admiration. He has confronted the challenges of a tumultuous family life and excelled in a diverse, international theatrical career; he lives each day with one of life's most dreaded diseases, yet faces tomorrow with joy, bravery and hope."

– Tina VanderHeyden, producer, Andrew Lloyd Webber's
THE PHANTOM OF THE OPERA

« • »

"Byron Nease should be our guide. What he has to say is true, moving, profound and most of all, entertaining. You'll come away asking, 'But how does he know me so well?' He knows us because, like us, he's been there. Bravo!"

– Linda Ellerbee, journalist "voice" of the New York Yankees

« • »

"A feast of inspiration!"

– Angela Lansbury, Tony Award-winning actress

« • »

"I know Byron Nease as a splendid singer – or, more precisely, as a singing actor who invariably uses his rich voice to project character, not just to float lovely sounds. I also know him as a tough and brave human being who has managed to triumph over daunting personal trials. He has done so, moreover, with rare insight, sensitivity and candor, not to mention self-deprecating wit. His story is instructive, also poignant."

– Martin Bernheimer, Pulitzer Prize-winning critic, author and lecturer

« • »

"Transcendent"

- Jane Pauley, journalist & broadcaster

"Byron Nease's story takes us from his fractured childhood as the son of a powerful preacher to his life in the theater and as a world class traveler. But it is the emotional terrain of his journey – his capacity to embrace life fully in the face of health challenges and loss – that offers the reader a truly captivating, valuable and intimate experience."

– Sally Fisher, author, activist and founder of Northern Lights Alternatives

«·»

"When I think of Byron Nease and his ability to move, inspire and motivate, there is one word that comes to mind: Exquisite."

– Karen Berg, CEO, CommCore Strategies

«·»

"If ever there was a person worthy of the name of 'survivor,' it is Byron Nease. This handsome, strapping Broadway star is not only a long-term survivor of a life-threatening illness, but survived a childhood filled with parental abuse and neglect. At a time in his life and career when most people would only have time for their own interests, Byron took his grandmother into his home, nursing her after three strokes. Byron's stories of hope and recovery are filled with heartfelt remembrances and humorous anecdotes."

– Mary Fisher, artist, author and AIDS activist

«·»

"Having known Byron Nease for more than 30 years, I am constantly amazed at his courage, his love of life, his artistic talent and his capacity for reinvention. This beautifully written and fascinating book is for all of us who sometimes need a kick in the pants to keep going, no matter what life throws at us."

– Suzyn Waldman, broadcaster and voice of the New York Yankees

«·»

"I have watched Byron Nease's story unfold over the past 15 years, both as a medical professional and as a friend. It's a remarkable story of strength, success, grace and inspiration; a straightforward account of how one man has dealt with challenge after challenge, facing more obstacles than any of us should ever have to. Nease's story resonates with us all – with those living with HIV infection and its treatment, but also with everyone who has had to overcome adversity in any form."

– Dr. Henry W. Murray, M.D., Arthur Ashe Professor of Medicine,
Weill Cornell Medical College

《•》

"There are many levels of virtuosity; in order to ascend to the highest level, one must know oneself. When I first came in contact with Byron Nease as a student, he had barely reached level one, but his gifts were obvious. He has become an inspiration to many students who have passed through my classroom over the past 25 years. He persevered even when the journey was not easy and his dedication to the development of his artistic expression has been an example. This book further demonstrates his commitment to sharing his gifts."

– Ben Bollinger, Byron Nease's college music professor

《•》

"Thank you, Byron Nease, for your words and your indomitable spirit. You never will know how many people have watched you persevere and have come to feel that they, too, can go on."

–Phil Hall, Broadway conductor, composer and producer

《•》

"What a read! What a ride! What a life!'

– Bonnie Franklin, actress

《•》

"Energy, tenacity, creativity, intelligence, humor and charm all come to mind when I think of Byron Nease. The many adversities he has successfully overcome during his life and his ability to integrate these strengths and experiences as an artist, writer and speaker render him a person whom all would do well to know."

– Roy Black, retired President of Johnson and Johnson, Inc

ACKNOWLEDGEMENTS

*I*t is clear to me that I am a composite of all my relationships, heritage and experience. Beyond that, I believe that we bring with us to this world our own unique spirit with lessons to be learned, needs to be met, adventures to behold.

I have had many teachers along the way. You know who you are... my family of friends who have loved me both because of and sometimes in spite of myself. You have supported me in every way possible and I am grateful more than words can express. Most of all, Mary, Scotty, Julie, VonAnn, Marilyn, Suzanne, Phil, Wesley, Brooks, Ginny, Ben, Caz, Rob, Bonnie, Suzyn, Joseph del Ponte and so many that are gone, but who live in my heart.

Most specifically, in regard to my writing, I wish to acknowledge Frances Weaver, Linda Ellerbee, Sally Fisher, Jim Heynen, Patti Edmund, Orval Nease, Wesley Eure, Peter McGowan, the late Jennifer Moyer; and my generously patient friends who have read draft after draft, endless letters and articles across the years and have saved this verbose, and sometimes vitriolic writer from himself time and again.

All of these have been the composers of my soul, and this book. Wisdom has found me both in the depths and at the pinnacles of my life ... it is my fondest desire that in my writing, sharing my experiences will serve to help others in the same situation know that they are not alone. It is different talking to someone in the boat rather than waving to them from shore.

Henry David Thoreau said "Most people live lives of quiet desperation." And while I believe that we are all called to the test, whether or not it may be at the moment we prefer, I prefer the sentiment in Jerry Herman's lyric, "There's a thank you, you can give life, when you live life... all the way!"

- for Fran -

BEHIND THE MASK... No More

PROLOGUE

On a cool Southern California morning, in a prosperous, citrus-scented suburb, a very attractive, very pregnant woman bolted from her white colonial. As she sped down the driveway in her pale green Cadillac convertible, a tall, red-faced man ran after, calling for her to stop. She paused at the foot of the drive and their verbal combat resumed – words that cut to the bone, and had all been said before.

My mother Ann, elegant and talented, had spent most of her life in mental anguish that frequently prompted "trips away" for rest, shock treatments and drug therapy. My father Orval, a third-generation Nazarene minister and pillar of the community, was once again trying to reason with her in an unreasonable situation. Conflict had displaced love as the constant in their relationship. The pregnancy was me.

More bitter words and my mother drove off, leaving my father in the exhaust of her anger, to Mt. San Antonio Hospital for my birth by caesarean section. I'd been conceived in hopes of saving this marriage that had gone wrong even before it began 14 years earlier.

For generations, my family history has read like a gothic novel. The cast of characters included fascinating, beautiful and brilliant people, viciously unstable ones – sometimes, one in the same. Their life stories brimmed with ambition and accomplishment, but also with scandal and disorder. Both of my parents inherited a legacy they would pass on to me: how to show the world one face, and conceal another.

I mastered this in life long before I had to affect it on stage, donning the mask of the Phantom. It was the only way I could reconcile being a pastor's son and an abused child; a gay man, in a family where homosexuality equaled damnation; a musical theater star expected to bare his soul on stage, but cloak his HIV-positive status to keep working.

As hard as I worked on concealment and denial, though, I kept running up against this truth: The secrets would not hold. The masks would not stay on.

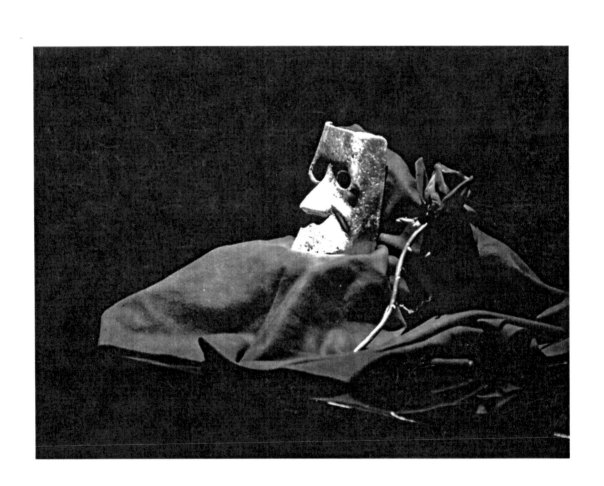

BEHIND THE MASK

*"Masquerade, paper faces on display; mask your face
so the world will never find you."*

– "Masquerade," *The Phantom of the Opera*, Andrew Lloyd Webber

After five years and 1,700 performances of playing Raoul, the love interest and valiant protector of Christine in Andrew Lloyd Webber's *The Phantom of the Opera*, I had the remarkable adventure of crossing into the dark side: playing the Phantom in the beautiful Kopit/Yeston Phantom production.

I've long believed that one reason many people are fascinated – even obsessed – with Gaston Leroux's timeless story is that we all have demons. We have a "good angel" and a "bad angel," each trying to get our ear as we wrestle with our needs, desires and obligations. With the Phantom, that disparity between light and dark is as clear as the mask on his face: pure white hiding dark disfigurement. He was brilliant, childish, loving, petulant, controlling, gifted, creative; blindingly alone, literally deformed and wanting desperately to be part of the world he could only observe at a distance.

By the time I joined the *Phantom* cast, I was accustomed to playing a wide variety of roles. But donning that mask, even during rehearsals, affected me deeply. The Phantom resonated with my history, especially its dark chapters. My deformities. My demons.

In my childhood, it was a regular state of being for seemingly irreconcilable things to be happening simultaneously. I was loved. I was abused. I was a child of blessing. I was a child in bondage. I was told I could accomplish anything. I was beaten and told I was worthless. I was told God loved me. I was told I was a sinner under the ever-present threat of eternal damnation. In between a few wonderful passages of living in a stable household with my Dad, I was bounced from home to home, parent to stepparent, among various sets of grandparents, aunts and uncles, in and out of military school and through more grammar schools that I care to remember.

And so I learned early on that we all wear masks – sometimes forced upon us, sometimes of our own devise, chosen out of fear, denial, self-protection. I had shown the world a false face, of one sort or another, for as long as I could remember. The first was the mask of "The Best Little Boy in the World."

Throughout my youth and teen years, though my hormones raged, I did my best to fit the mold I knew to be acceptable at home, at school and especially in church. But as my voice and performance skills grew stronger, my soul became more restless. This, I never whispered aloud. The mask that denied my sexuality became harder to sustain. When I finally moved to New York, I shed that mask with joy and fervor – and it was not long before I had to share the reality of who I truly was with those I loved the most, my family on the West Coast.

The news was met with varying degrees of dismay, shock, relief and angry, pious righteousness. It became clear that the three thousand mile geographical distance was a wise choice both personally and professionally. I had to define my own values while being authentic with those I loved. All other avenues were filled with even greater pitfalls and complications. "The Best Little Boy in the World" mask was shattered forever. Quite suddenly I became, in many ways, a stranger to those with whom I'd been raised. There was far more separating us than the geographical. Our distances were political, social, spiritual and philosophical. In my strange and wonderful new world, a theatrical realm short on stability and long on self-indulgence, I began a new journey. I was forging my way, mask free.

My face might just as well have been shattered into the many pieces of the masks I'd worn as I began to balance the values I held to be true with the barrage of new and different philosophies swirling around me. I became swept up in the movement toward transformational thinking, diving into the unfamiliar waters eagerly. My bedroom began to look like a self-help library as I questioned the basic premise of my life without the religious guilt that had always been present. I began to understand that I was responsible for my own life and no longer wanted to spend it in anguish over my childhood. I learned to take back my own power and believe I was worthy of success and having a whole life. It was the beginning of a long and important process. I was thrilled and horrified at the tug-of-war I felt inside.

On stage masks were still required, both literally and symbolically. Some fit better than others. Finding the places inside of me that would resonate with various roles became a powerful professional tool; for the most part, I learned to leave those masks at the stage door.

Until *Phantom.* Originally, I was hired to play the young love interest, Raoul. This was a part not so far from whom I was at that time in my life. But when I officially learned I was HIV-positive in 1990, I went into a new closet, donned a new mask. Part of it was self-preservation. Part of it was professional. But most of all,

I had to have time to make my peace with the implications of a diagnosis that, in those days, was tantamount to a death sentence. I had to deal with my mortality. I had to decide what I valued and how I wanted to live my life, whatever was left of it. I had to decide whom to tell, how and when. For two years, my status was known only to my doctor, my lover, my accountant, my shrink, three friends and my leading ladies (there was kissing involved and in those days, who knew?). No one else.

Over time, I told a wider group of friends and colleagues, then my sisters. I had not intended to tell my parents. I thought, "Why worry them?" But the mother of a friend whose son had died gave me a different perspective. "Wouldn't it be better for them to find out while you are strong and healthy," she suggested, "rather than to learn by seeing you in a sick bed?" And so I made the trek to California to reveal my greatest secret so far to the people I'd loved the longest.

My sisters, Joan and Sharon, were both emotional, but were completely supportive. I took Sharon with me to tell Mother, not knowing who'd need the support more, Mother or me. But in that moment, this woman who had been a source of uncertainty my entire life became the mother of my dreams. As we both cried, she put her arms around me and said, "Well, these are the hands that brought you into the world. And if need be, these are the hands that will hold you when you leave." It could not, despite our sadness and uncertainty, have been a finer response and affirmation. It was her finest moment in my recollection.

Next came my dad and stepmother. I arranged to go with them to the mountains for a weekend, and packed my luggage with books and information about HIV/AIDS. They already knew about my friend Mary Fisher, who had gone public with her HIV-positive status, speaking at the 1992 Republican National Convention. They were terribly fond of Mary and, by then, knew of Magic Johnson's status as well – but they could have no idea of what I'd come across the country to share with them.

We had a very nice cabin amidst the tall trees ... my Dad has always loved the mountains. As many times as I had rehearsed the disclosure in my mind, I don't remember the words I spoke. I do remember the silence that followed, and the tears. I gave them the history of the two years since I'd found out. It was a bittersweet time of affirming our love, digesting all of the information I'd brought with me to share, and considering the implications. All in all, under the circumstances, I thought it was a good weekend.

I flew immediately back to New York for a concert date. I'll never forget walking into my apartment, putting down my bags and hitting the PLAY button on my answering machine. The first message was from Dad. He said he hoped that his emotional reaction to my disclosure was OK and not out of proportion. He said that I was enormously valuable to him – and that he hated to see my life so devastated "by having made such bad choices." And so another mask was donned. This one, the mask of silence.

After that, I told my stepsisters, Cindy and Carolyn. I knew it would have been difficult for them to withhold this information from Dad and my stepmother, Jean, and didn't want to put them in that situation. Carolyn, while upset, was wonderful and fully supportive. Across the years we had developed a deep and abiding affection and connection that was punctuated with visits by her and her son. The death of her daughter Tracy some years before had brought us even closer together. Her gregarious spirit and willingness to participate in my life meant the world to me. And just as I had been present for some of her challenges, she vowed to see me through mine.

Cindy and I had drifted apart across the years. Though we'd been inseparable in high school, my move to New York, her marriage and children and, most significantly, the revelation that I was gay created a distance that surprised and disappointed me. But it was as it was, and she had already let me know in no uncertain terms that I was to be allowed no "alone time" or personal access to her sons and daughter. Though all my other nieces, nephew and godchildren had come for visits and spent wonderful times with me in my home or in the places in which I was performing, Cindy stated clearly that she was responsible for the morals of her children and did not think my "lifestyle" was acceptable for them. The news that I was HIV-positive opened an even greater chasm between us. I believe we all lost in this decision. And so, another mask was bestowed, the mask of unworthiness.

Although I had begun to open up about my sexuality, being HIV-positive drove me back behind a mask of silence, afraid for my career. After I left *Phantom*, I began a stint performing on luxury cruise ships on the high seas and was advised that if my sexuality were discussed or my health status known, I would not be allowed the opportunity to travel as I wished. At that point, believing I had such a limited time left, I decided, selfishly, to conceal my situation and take the opportunity (perhaps my last) to see the world.

Off the ships, my authenticity to the people in my world had widened to almost everyone I knew. I was more and more public both about being gay and HIV-positive, doing speaking events and benefits; I even created a one-man performance designed for traditional houses of worship, called *From the Parsonage to Broadway*. In that show, I sang and spoke about what it's like to grow up gay in the church, the spiritual ramifications of it as well as the ostracism that too often accompanies it and about being HIV-positive. But mostly, in show, I celebrated diversity and what I believe as divine truth: That as children of a truly merciful God, we are all loved, no matter what. The lessons of Grace.

Over time, I've learned to surrender all my masks – to uncover, to come clean. It's an enormous relief. When showing myself to those around me, I no longer look for approval, just authenticity.

In many ways, HIV was a gift in that it forced me to rip off my masks and go to my core. From the time I was a small boy, I'd been praised for being cute, for my voice and being able to carve a career with it. I had the appearance of affluence, the demeanor of a winner. And no matter how thin the veneer, my mask in my early professional years was one of invincibility, of having it together, of pride.

After many years of bombarding my system with drugs to save my life, the side effects became brutal: a deforming skeletal wasting in my face, a hump on my back, and a dryness in my throat that caused me to lose my voice totally on two very public occasions and rarely be certain of what audiences would hear. Whatever confidence I had, in every area, was stripped.

And so there came a time when not only did I have to accept the help of others, but I had to redefine my value as a human being. I had to believe, really believe, that not only was I not a statistic, but that I am more than my voice. I am more than the face I no longer recognized. Everything by which I had defined myself was taken. When you are stripped of all the essentials that people take for granted, you are left with the most of who you are. I had to look at what was left. Just me. Just my heart. Just my mind, my integrity, my values.

Later, as I sought help to repair what the drugs had done to my voice, body and face, it was not a matter of putting on masks, but simply regaining a semblance of my physical identity. It was more than not wanting to look ill, or old before my time: more than putting on another mask of "acceptability" or attractiveness upon which my value was based. I just needed to look like me again.

When you put on a mask, you take on its mantle. That's the price. Masks are not necessary when there is nothing to hide. That's where I am today. No more masks. No more secrets. Just me, content to dispense with all the masks and show the face of a survivor.

"Masquerade, paper faces on display, mask your face so the world will never find you…"

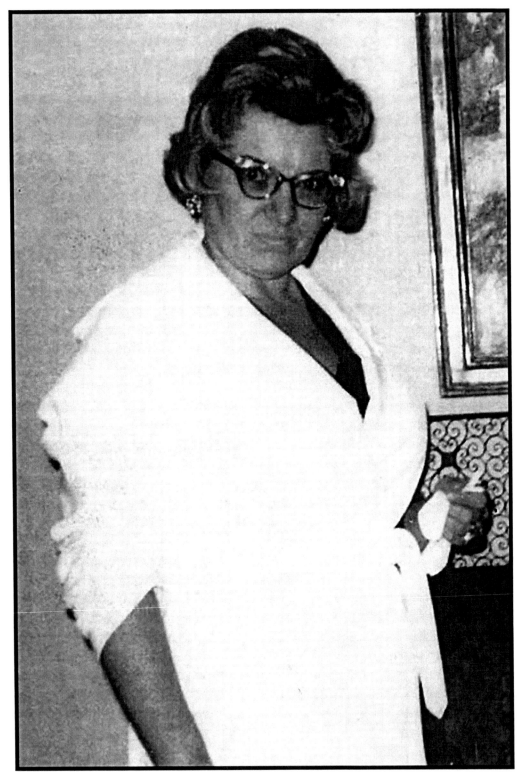

Mother
The face of my childhood...

MOTHER

*"I'll be loving you, Always, with a love that's true, Always
… days may not be fair, Always. That's when I'll be there,
Always. Not for just an hour. Not for just a day.
Not for just a year, but Always." – "Always," Irving Berlin*

t is her music I remember most of all. My earliest memories of my mother are of her voice. She had a magnificent soprano: rich, vibrant, strong and pure.

When I was a little boy, we sang together, around the house, in the car, all the time. If I was naughty…if she was upset…when life was rough… I knew that if I could just get her to sing, everything would be okay.

But mostly, things were not okay. Though she was brilliant, beautiful, talented and ambitious, my mother struggled with a chemical imbalance her entire life. A psychic once described her as "someone who is covered with blisters – she can't stand to touch or be touched, though she wants both desperately."

But Ann – Mother – always had demons. She had to compete for her own mother's attention with that of her mentally retarded sister, the demands of the L.A. Department of Water and Power, where my grandmother was Financial Controller, not to mention the world of café society that Eva (Granny) increasingly inhabited. She also had to contend with a sporadically present father who had remarried, and become far more interested in his newborn son than his talented and beautiful daughter. And his eldest child, to him, no longer existed.

Through it all, my mother's one salvation was her music. From adolescence, she was an emerging talent with a wonderful mezzo soprano, highly developed at an early age. When she performed, all of her uncertainty fell away. Singing and dancing at an early age with the likes of Judy Garland and Shirley Temple, she substituted the adoration of audiences for the love missing from her family.

She had no models for normalcy or dependability. She lived in a world of uncertainty – of constantly shifting boundaries, egos, life circumstances and values. No wonder, then, that her mother's celebrity marriage in 1940 sent her into a tailspin. David Hutton was famous because of his career as a Vaudeville head-liner – and infamous because his first wife was Aimee Semple McPherson, the sensationally controversial evangelist.

Mother was staying with a girlfriend when she heard about her mother's wedding – on the radio. Though mother's father Andrew had remarried, he became furious when her mother, Eva, did so; and, in a fit of jealous rage, instituted custody proceedings.

It was a much celebrated case, not just because of the notoriety of the players, but because Andrew only sought custody of Ann – not of Alice, the daughter with mental challenges. The judge in the custody case raked Andrew over the coals. The newspaper clippings looked like something out of a television movie of the week.

To escape the furor, my mother was enrolled in a private girls' academy on the campus of Pasadena Nazarene College. There, she became a singing sensation and star on campus. And in her sophomore year of high school, she met a college junior named Orval Nease Jr. – the man who would become her husband, and my father.

Orval was handsome and electric. He was always front and center, whether on the church platform or on the pitcher's mound. He was the crowned prince of the Nazarene Church, a religious dynasty of sorts, because his own father, Orval Sr., had been president of the college and gone on to become the church's General Superintendent – kind of like the pope of the denomination. Charismatic and gifted, young Orval showed all the promise that was expected of him.

Mother was wildly in love with him, I think, until the day she died. At first, they seemed to be well-suited, both in spiritual goals and in their shared ability to move people: he with his spirited preaching and she with her exquisite singing.

Two years later, with a mixed sense of love and honor, they were married. In the wedding photo, they look like two Dresden dolls, delicate, perfect and without a hint of the turmoil already boiling beneath the surface. The wedding was a grand affair, lavish, well-attended, the picture of propriety, elegance and style. Blessed by the church and in the presence of hundreds of witnesses, their life together as husband and wife began. One of the saddest things I've ever heard is when my dad told me, decades later: "When I saw her coming down the aisle, I knew I was making the mistake of my life."

Ann Leach

From: <byronnease@aol.com>
To: <EPML@aol.com>
Sent: Thursday, February 12, 2009 3:56 PM
Subject: My first real review …

AND … WWW.BYRONNEASE.COM IS UP!

BEHIND THE MASK… No More
BookSurge (180 pp.)
$20.00 paperback
November 10, 2008
ISBN: 978-1-4196-5529-6

Springing from conservative roots in Southern California, Nease's adolescence is the first time he'scompelled to don a mask—his burgeoning sexuality creates a secret divide between him, his Nazareneminister father and the rest of his family. Hiding behind a carefully choreographed portrayal of the boysociety expects him to be, the author taps into acting talent that eventually=2 0leads him to New York and a career in the theater.

Finally comfortable with himself, Nease reveals his true face to everyone in his life andsaves his masquerading for the stage. His career highlights include a role in Angela Lansbury's revival of *Mame* and, crucial to the memoir's mask motif, both Andrew Lloyd Weber's *The Phantom of the Opera* andMaury Yeston's *Phantom*. When he is diagnosed with HIV, however, he finds himself wearing a new mask and must once again find the strength to show the world his true self. Because of its strong thematic backbone—and sometimes in spite of it—Nease's memoir is a success.

While the idea of a gay man spending his life behind "masks" may come off as cliché, Nease's having played the romantic lead in Weber's *Phantom* and the grotesque antihero in Yeston's version lends an unexpected sincerity to the book. The narrative, delivered in a calm, meditative voice, oscillates between serious life analysis and fond recollection of theatrical triumphs. Not everything fits cleanly into the maskmotif, but when employed correctly, it is highly effective. The story of one man's struggle to find inner peace, the book is an incisive look at the joys and hardships of a career in theater—but its quiet universality elevates it to an essential portrait of unwavering stamina and inspiring heart.

A meaningful memoir.

My parents moved to their first pastorate, a small congregation in Little Rock, Arkansas. Years later, my mother recalled making a loving, if difficult and ill-informed, attempt at domesticity and being a preacher's wife. She would sing solos before he preached and, as she put it, "stood by him as best I could." But the problems between them were evident early on. Ann was not emotionally equipped as a help-mate; life as a pastor's wife was alien and rigid compared to her worldly and glamorous upbringing. She was still a volatile child herself. And so, my dad was learning to distance himself from her outrageous behavior and burying himself in the work of the church. But things were out of control, and my father relinquished his pastorate.

Mother and Dad

Dad went into the army for two years after which he worked for U.S. Rubber Company and continued his studies at the University of Southern California. After some time had passed, he was given his second pastorate, in Santa Barbara, California.

By now, there were two daughters, Joan and Sharon. My father was once again successful in his ministry, and the church grew steadily – but so did mother's mental instability. Both because of her medical bills and her over-spending, the family could not survive on his modest, minister's salary and the means of the congregation. Both my mother's parents (separately and unbeknownst to the other) subsidized the household, but the finances still were disastrous. Mother adored her father. Orval, however never could win his favor – and the rift between husband and father exacerbated her mental and emotional problems. Ann and Orval became pawns in a tug of war between her relatives, his relatives and the church.

Sanitariums, drug therapy, shock treatments, psychiatrists, prayer circles, exorcisms; nothing could relieve the imbalance. Everyone was sad, Mother most of all. But the preacher's family had to appear perfect, so all of the family secrets – especially her erratic behavior – stayed locked within the propriety of the parsonage.

For the next pastorate, in Ontario, California, the parsonage was to be an apartment attached to the church. But because it was judged unworthy and not fit for my mother by her father – and because the family desperately needed some distance between church premises and their troubles – my grandfather bought our family a beautiful house: a pillared, white colonial. It was to this house – beautiful on its face, tumultuous within – that I was born.

My parents hoped, and my grandparents expected, that I would somehow save this marriage that had gone wrong almost from the beginning. No pressure there.

My sisters Joan and Sharon, then seven and nine, greeted this new arrival as a mixed blessing. They were made to dress up, stand before our father's congregation and offer the birth announcement. Sharon recalls that they were not amused.

The first few years of my life were punctuated with Mother's suicide attempts, continued "trips away" for shock therapy and all other forms of chemical treatment – and, finally, the end of their tragically dysfunctional union. I was four, sitting with Dad, Joan and Sharon at the breakfast table. Mother, suffering greatly with the emotional hangover of yet another suicide attempt, staggered downstairs and, in her silent rage, smashed two glass milk bottles over Dad's head.

I'm not sure if I remember the chaos that followed or if I've just heard the story so many times that it seems as if I do. But there was a great deal of blood from Dad's injury and, this was the final incident. Later that day, she called my

This rather amazing photo was taken just before my birth. The fact
that it was cut in half is poignantly prophetic…

grandmother and a moving company, stripped the house of most of its possessions and left with me. Sharon still smarts at the memory of seeing our mother
drive off, leaving her standing in the driveway.

Mother and I moved into a guest house behind the home of my grandmother
Eva and her second husband, in the small community of Toluca Lake. Mother
embarked on a new career, following her mother's footsteps in the world of finance. By this time, Eva – Granny to me – had retired as the Financial Controller
for the Los Angeles Department of Water and Power and was free to take care
of me while Mother went back to school and started work at Bank of America,
right across the street from Warner Brothers Studios. Shortly thereafter, she and
Casey Stengel opened Valley National Bank.

As mother worked her way up the corporate ladder in various financial in-
stitutions, her personal demons subsided … somewhat. She no longer had the
pressure of husband, church, three children and all that had been expected of
her. My time was spent mostly with Granny and Gramp, with the odd visit to Dad.
At some point Granny convinced Mother that we'd all be better off if I went to
live with Dad, so I did for four years.

When I was in the midst of third grade, Mother sued for my custody, and I entered the most turbulent period of my young life. As she worked, I spent much of my time on the road shuttled between her, Dad, various sets of grandparents and aunts and uncles. I can't remember all the names of the schools I attended. The physical and emotional abuse is hard for me to describe even now. But the bruises on my body were nothing compared to the scars in my heart and soul. As is often the case with abused children, my instincts were to deny what was happening and cover for my mother, even as she subjected me to extraordinary mental cruelty and tremendous physical violence.

She regularly beat me, often with a metal shoe-horn (which Sharon and I found, going through her home after her death). Once when I was in fifth grade, she threw me down the staircase of our home because I had made the egregious error of eating a cheeseburger with Gramp after school, and was not hungry for dinner. Later that night, I got on my bike and rode in the rain (my trusty Boy Scout flashlight in hand) to Granny and Gramp's house a few miles away. Granny dried me off, put me to bed, called Mother and insisted I stay there for the night. Mother would have none of it.

Within an hour, Granny's house was surrounded by the local police. From behind the floodlights trained on the house, a policeman on his loud-speaker demanded: "Release the boy!" I was terrified, knowing what awaited me. But Granny had no choice. She wrapped me in a blanket and walked me down the winding brick walkway to the open arms of my mother, who was crying convincingly and thanking the policemen profusely. We were taken back to our home – and I got the beating of my life. I could not go to school for a few days until the bruising subsided, and was left with a strict warning that I was never to see Granny and Gramp. We never spoke of that incident again.

After that, for more than a year my only contact with Granny and Gramp was when they would come by the schoolyard while I was in the "after school program" for the children of working parents and we'd visit through the chain link fence. Finally, Granny sent a new Lincoln Continental, Mother relented, and I was once again allowed to be with them after school.

So much drama around a boy's simple desire to be with grandparents. So much vitriol to discredit my dad and keep me from seeing him. So many beatings and episodes of abuse – from being threatened with kitchen knives to being locked out of the house –alternating with an almost smothering physicality when she was lonely. Over time, I developed a deep distrust of any woman who showed me affection. Although I had Granny, even she, probably in an effort to make up for Mother's abuse, was overwhelming in her affection. Though I already knew I was gay, I also knew there were appropriate and fulfilling ways for me to relate to women – but I had no such relationships until I went to live with my dad and his second wife Jean. If I have any healthy trust of the women in my life, it is because of the unconditional and (at last) appropriate love of my stepmother.

Mom (Jean) and Me

When I was in junior high school, Mother married a colleague from the bank where she worked. I remember thinking, as she walked down the aisle, "Please God, let this just be a bad dream." It was, quite literally, a bloody nightmare – a tempestuous and violent marriage, in which we both were abused. After two years, it ended in divorce. By this time I was once again living with Dad, and Mother could devote all her time and energy to her career. And she did well.

Whatever her personal dilemmas, she managed to succeed in her work. She was smart and commanding, elegant and vivacious, an excellent manager. Now living in Beverly Hills, she thrived as a vice-president of one of the largest private savings and loan corporations in the world. She was on the board at the Music Center in Los Angeles and was instrumental in starting the Chamber Music Society there. Mother helped raise millions of dollars for charity, and sat on boards and committees that filled her lonely hours.

As I grew in years and confidence, I attempted to get beyond the abuse and forge a relationship with Mother on my terms. Some wounds, though, seem never to heal completely. As a young adult, on a particular Thanksgiving I was kneeling in front of my grandmother's mahogany buffet putting away a platter. Mother reached down to help and I automatically put my hand up to shield my face. Mother got it instantly and burst into tears. We did not speak of it that day, but a few weeks later, she and I had a conversation where she asked me to describe my childhood. I will always remember her tears as she apologized and said, "I don't remember it that way." And whether she did or not, at that moment I was able to forgive her. I would never forget what we all went through. But after four years of not speaking to her during my high school years, I knew it was worse for me and for her to have no communication at all. So I told her two things: that I would always tell her the truth, and I would never walk away. It was more for me than for her, but it opened a door that otherwise would have forever remained shut.

After her retirement, she married one more time. Ed Switzer was her husband and (unhappy) companion for nine years until she died on New Year's Eve in 1999. It was a shock for us all. Mother was such a survivor, I think we all just assumed that she'd live forever. But in those years she created for them a beautiful home. Her love of the arts extended beyond music. My mother loved beautiful things ... so many beautiful things! She had always taken pride and pleasure in making a beautiful environment. I remember one purchase in particular: Passing a gallery, she saw a beautiful painting of an Italian landscape, and in no time we were loading it into the back of her Lincoln Continental. I remember asking her, "How are you going to pay for that?" She smiled and said, "A dollar now, and a dollar when they catch me!"

Mother was always an early riser and it was not unusual for me to stumble sleepily from my room to find a house that did not remotely resemble the one I'd seen the night before, but had been completely rearranged. And I am my mother's son in that: My own obsession to create and live in a beautiful environment, I owe to her. I think she felt, as I do, that this is one thing over which one can exert some control, in a world which otherwise seems so uncertain.

I find it ironic that the health decline that led to Mother's death began after she tripped on one of the many layers of luxurious carpets decorating her home. I find irony, too, in the fact that a woman so astute in her business died without a will, so her precious things went to a man who had no appreciation for their provenance, history and sentiment. Ed kept everything at Mother's death, and when he died, everything went to his sons, including a large financial inheritance from her father; the worst insult of all was taking the jewelry she wore in her casket … never found. After trying for four years, Sharon and I still recovered only a portion of what we could prove was hers before their marriage. Her negligence in this felt like Mother's final act of not taking care of her children.

Mother, like most of us, was a study in contrasts. She could be warm and funny and had the capacity for an almost childlike silliness that could be delightful, or disconcerting, when it punctuated an otherwise troubled demeanor. Mother was astute and angry, afraid and covetous, bright and self-destructive. She remained, however, in her own way, a seeker of all things bright and beautiful … a seeker of love … a seeker of God and His Grace.

Till the day she died, she struggled with her demons. And yet despite her capacity for brutality, no one in my world has ever touched me in quite the same way, or has made me feel so completely loved, understood and appreciated for *all* of who I am. This woman was, as the psychic said, "covered in blisters, longing to touch and be touched." It is a touch I will miss till the end of my days.

In the last years of her life, we were able to make peace with many of the uncertainties and unhappy memories. And I credit us both with that. It was hard

work and took much forgiveness and compassion on both parts. But when she died, there was nothing left unsaid. She would leave messages on my voicemail that I now wish I'd kept – some of them singing, all of them telling me how much I meant to her. In my quarter-century career as a singer, I have had many teachers who taught me notes, precision, tone quality, enunciation, musical line and form – but it was Mother who taught me to sing from my heart.

When I was a little boy, I would tell her "I love you twenty-hundreds!" because that was the biggest number I could think of. Today, there is no measure for the volume of feeling I hold. I know that twenty-hundred angels have heard a new voice in their ranks, the most beautiful one of all, leading them in song.

Mother, in better days

FATHERS, SONS AND GRANDSONS

"Like a tree he'll grow, with his head held high, and his feet planted firm on the gorund ..."

– Rogers & Hammerstein - *Carousel*

My Father and I
April, 1957

Make no mistake, my father loves me. When I look in his eyes I see love, appreciation and gratitude. Maybe even a little bit of admiration for my willingness to be authentic. But I also see sadness and disappointment. As much as he has shown his love across the years, I believe he would have preferred or been more comfortable with a different son.

Not just for him, but for me. That I have lived my adult life without a traditional family of my own – specifically, a wife – is disconcerting and of concern for him. In his relationship with Jean, he has found the greatest joy, peace and fulfillment of his life. I know he wants the same for me. He is also concerned for my eternal welfare.

Gratefully, I have loved well and been loved well. It's just in a different way from the one in which I was raised, and the one he'd hoped for, for me.

In 1977 I fell in love for the first time, big-time. In all other areas, I had a wonderfully open relationship with my family, especially Dad and Jean. So after at time it seemed dishonest not to include them in what was a major component of my life. I determined that a lie of omission was still a lie and decided to come out to my family about my sexuality and my relationship.

"Often in error … never in doubt" – Fran Weaver

I guess I was naïve. I practiced what I'd say with my sisters and my mother – and when I said it, they were great. Then I made a special trip to Los Angeles to speak with my dad. After all, it felt as if I was married and no one knew. I was tired of editing half my story or changing the gender references when I described my life with my friends.

We went out for breakfast, and I said my practiced piece. His first reaction was as I'd hoped: He said he loved me and nothing would change that. I thought we were on a good track. A few weeks later I was back in New York, flying out the door to an audition, when I stopped by the mailbox, saw a letter from Dad and opened it. His words were so provocative that not only did I miss my subway stop and the audition, but found myself in Battery Park, practically catatonic on a park bench, utterly overwhelmed by what I'd just read. Covered in emotional soot.

The following two letters are the one my dad wrote and my response (after many tears and even more hours at my typewriter). I've always been grateful that Dad agreed to let his letter to be published in a book by my friend and mentor, Dr. Rob Eichberg, called *Coming Out: An Act of Love*.

Dear Bud,

You are on my mind and heart these days so much of the time that I must sit down and express my thoughts. Four months ago you took me into your confidence expressing your choice to engage in homosexual activities as a major integral part of your life commitment ... of your sexual lifestyle. I accept the openness and painfulness of your special confidence with love and understanding because you are my son. You reached me with more shocking and painful impact than anything I have ever experienced. To know of your involvement is the saddest, most disappointing news that I have ever received.

I have empathized with your hurt ... with your deep turmoil since your earliest years as a boy ... with your excruciating uncertainty about your masculinity ... with many years of discrediting experiences you have suffered as well as your dad's credibility.

I have admired your courage and persistence ... in swimming, singing, and acting ... in your studying, working and growing with responsibility, in your compassion for others and your desire for excellence. You are an immensely valuable human being. But submitting to these tendencies, to these inner leanings, to these latent, sexual dissatisfactions ... you are giving yourself to the distortion of the natural human process, to the unhealthiest of an immorality that is as ancient as mankind and clearly warned against as sodomy in both the Old Testament and the New Testament.

Despite the experiences and associations that you have had across these recent years, you can change the balance. Never believe in never! By total humbleness of desire you can work through these human tensions ... and discover your maximum possibilities through yielding yourself to the divine tensions of seeking God's will.

Bud, you acquired through your heritage and your early development a positive, spiritual sensitivity that is a gift from God. The greatest thrill and hopefulness of your life can be realized by taking the steps necessary to sever your relationships with a process that will inevitably become a binding, twisting, narrowing, self-destroying force within you ... and seek the help of someone who will guide you into a Christ-ethic that will once again open your life to success and happiness and serenity.

You have an inner drive to succeed that is God given, but you will only make it by admitting to yourself this inner perversion of the fundamental process of successful fulfillment and, by redirecting your life to Matthew 6:33 ... "Seek ye first the Kingdom of God and His Righteousness, and all these things shall be added unto you."

The seeking is the drive ... that can be the most exciting, challenging, rewarding, fulfilling, motivator that you can imagine!

Bud, God has a plan for your life ,,, that He wants to accomplish ... through ... in spite of ... and because of all the influences that have been brought to bear on your life ... If you will accept His vision for your life ... He will multiply many times over what you give to Him ... and unfold in front of you a future of service and accomplishment and personal satisfaction for the next 26 years plus that will be astounding.

Although there are many, many scriptures especially in the Apostle Paul's writing that can assist you … initially following the progression of these words of Jesus in Matthew can be productive: 6:8, 33:7, 7, 14, 21:8:3;11:28, 12:33-37; 16:24;18:3, 22:37;23:12.

Bud, my deep love for you has prompted me to pour out my heart and mind and life experience to you in this letter … dedicated to the supreme worth that God has granted to you … and the gigantic, positive, possibilities that you can discover dedicating your life to doing His will.

I am always with you in the strength and caring and hoping and loving and seeking. Dad

Dear Dad and Mom,

I have so much to say to you. First and foremost is that I love you. I would never have begun this process last October had it not come from total love, trust and the desire to share with you all of who I am.

For a long time, my whole life, I have hidden and suppressed a part of me. The last three years, no, the last 26, has been a process for me of finding out all about who I am, dealing with it, and even learning to enjoy and capitalize on it. I suspect that I am still in that process. In fact, from all I have learned it seems this is a process that never ends. I believe we are always in the process of transformation, both when we consciously are aware of it and seeking it, and when we are not.

In this letter I have several objectives. Most importantly is to share with you so that you will know me more fully and have a wider foundation of information. Some of this, Dad, I shared with you in October. I want you both to know about my life experiences, my dreams, my hopes, my fears, my strengths, my weaknesses and all the information I have gathered. I hope that I can ease some of your fears and perhaps misconceptions about a world that is foreign to you.

While there are a few specific things from your letter of February 3ʳᵈ to which I wish to respond; generally, I do not wish to debate with you. I cannot make anything wrong or right, good or bad for you. And you cannot for me. What I can do is share my experience with you so that hopefully your frame of reference will be widened.

I received your letter, Dad, and experienced our conversation, Mom, with the grateful knowledge and special sense that we will walk through this together. Believe me, if this were not the case, I would have made a different choice entirely last fall.

The primary reason I did not share this with you previously was a fear of rejection. And our relationship is very important to me. I have learned to love and value our spe-

cial communication across the years and look forward to more. I respect you, I love you, and I value your opinions highly.

I could more easily have gone on indefinitely with the deception I had propagated for some time … the half-truths, the partial lies, the withheld communication. And I chose not to. I am at a place in my life where I do not have room for or energy to spend on that. Not with you.

Literally, for as long as I can remember being, I have known a different kind of need and desire for physical closeness and satisfaction than you experience. My most natural preference and satisfaction comes from expressing myself with and to another man. The only way I know to share this certainty with you is to compare it to your need and desire for physical sharing with someone of the opposite sex, of Orv and Jean.

Of course, as a boy, I did not realize all the ramifications of my instincts and feelings. But know they were there, even then. The only reason I stress that is because I want you to know that this is not something that I have chosen at random as something new, or different, or kinky or chic; it is a natural, normal part of my function as a human being, and always has been.

Growing up with this knowledge is difficult, at best. There is very little support in the world for gay people. Although it does get easier and better and more acceptable all the time, it still is a difficult path. While both the American Medical Association and American Convention of Psychiatrists have long since taken homosexuality off the books as an illness, aberration or anything abnormal, many people with less or limited information retain old prejudice and ill feeling. As in anything, fear of the unknown often results in denial and hostility.

I know that to be true for me. Really, until I was in college I denied my gayness, lied about it, was afraid of it and in short did about everything but deal with it. I was making myself miserable with a double life by living one thing and feeling quite another. It has only been in the past two years that I have come to terms with who I am and how to live constructively and responsibly with that. I feel free, serene, content and happy. I live one day at a time with as much creativity, intelligence and honor as I can muster.

As in the work I have chosen, I must create my own social structure, my own order because there do not seem to be many good gay role models for me, or at least ones I can relate to. Not that my life is about my sexuality. Hopefully … certainly, my world is larger than that. But that part of my life is constantly new frontier, for me as a man and for gay society in the world.

Dad, you mentioned at one point my "excruciating uncertainty about my own masculinity as well as my early unsure-ness about my Dad's credibility." One thing you both might be interested to know is that I have never been more certain about my masculinity, about what I have to offer both inside the bedroom and out. I think at times my sexuality was at issue. But sexuality and masculinity are two different issues. Secondly, I do not want to get stuck in the 'whys' of who I am, nor do I want you to. Be it genetic, or learned behavior for whatever set of reasons or circumstances, I am who I am. There is no fault or blame. It simply is. And the most consideration is acceptance and dealing with the truth.

Again, please know that this is not a tendency, an inner leaning, or latent sexual dissatisfaction. It is not a distortion of my most natural human tension. It is the most natural, fulfilling and satisfying way I know to express my sexuality. Keep in mind that I have had some experience with women as well. The binding, twisting, narrowing, self-destroying forces in me were in control only when I denied, lied about and was afraid to be fully who I am. The Christ ethic you talk about I believe to be working in my life as I do my best to express the love I have for myself and others with openness, generosity, compassion and responsibility.

There are many stereotypes of gay men I am sure you have seen. Unfortunately, what is most widely publicized is not at all my experience. It is a part of the gay world, but certainly not all of it . For me, being gay is simply loving someone of the same sex. Extreme behavior is not a part of my being. The Bud I am with you, is the Bud I am all the time.

One of the most difficult considerations for me to work through has been the uncertainty of the spiritual dimension of this issue. Clearly, I was raised to believe that homosexuality is a sin. And I had great concern for my eternal welfare. The struggle between what I'd been told and how I had been instructed scripturally versus my own instincts and sense of right and wrong was devastating.

One very positive result of this confrontation with both of you was that it finally forced me to look deep into my heart, soul and mind and well as seek some professional assistance to some very spiritual questions. I have spoken with three men, one of whom is a Catholic priest, one a Lutheran minister and the third is Ed Powers, who co-authored the enclosed study on Human Sexuality for The United Church of Christ. All three offered essentially the same verdict: that I am on solid ground, that this will be the major issue for the church in the 80s, and that what is important scripturally, socially and morally is how I deal with who I am. So the criteria is that I show love, caring responsibility, compassion and respect for and to those with whom I am involved, and not that it is specifically a man or a woman. Of course, there will be as many interpretations as there are denominations, people and insecurities.

Again, I cannot make this or anything else right or wrong for you. My intention has been to share more of me … all of me … so that we learn to live together with dignity, compassion, pride and full expression in all parts of our lives.

While I feel it's been necessary to go into some detail, all of this should be held in the context and perspective that my sexuality is only one area, one part of my life. And now you have it all.

I could have withheld this, and I chose to share. Thank you for giving me the space to feel free and safe. I love you both very much and hope that this letter with the enclosed books will help us all down the road to better understanding and richer, fuller relationships.

Bud

This began a correspondence that continued for many years. He sent me a copy of the book The Healing of the Homosexual. I sent him a copy of Loving Someone Gay. Many letters back and forth – this from 1989:

My Son,

I do not believe that you are congenitally homosexual. It is not an essential characteristic of your nature. It is an illusory picture of what you really are. It is an evolvement of the distorted thoughts and feelings that took form during those earliest fears, pains and convolutions after your birth.

You were born into an incredibly painful emotional turmoil in the climactic years of the tragically dysfunctional marriage experienced by your mother and me. Your first two years were laced with strife, upset and lack of peacefulness, harmony and assurance. At three years of age, you were taken from your sisters and me, only to become totally engulfed in a devastatingly unbalanced, smothering unhealthy climate of mother-daughter power struggle and self-indulgence, along with an intentional and most damaging counter-productive negative male imaging. Your subconscious was daily programmed with confusing, distorted pictures of the normal ingredients of love and intelligence.

Whatever interactions took place in those earliest forgotten years of your life between a totally vulnerable baby boy and two powerfully self-centered women, one with particularly irrational and violent behavior, will never be fully articulated.

But you became the victim of a female love-hate ego struggle, plus an overpowering derisive and ridiculing attitude toward males, that included at least one grandfather, stepfather and your Dad, and that inevitably created distorted perceptions about your own identity in relationship to both men and women.

It is well established that a Dad's role is the primary influence in the child's psycho-sexual image in the earliest years. You were robbed of that normal opportunity and were given the Dad-image of inadequacy, unreliability, distance and confusion. You had no chance to experience the modeling of a normal, loving father-son relationship.

You may painfully remember the confusingly negative climate that ravaged your conscious and unconscious mind during those years. You were denied the confident intimacy of a loving, supporting, caring picture of your Dad. It took you many years to develop any semblance of a relaxed feeling of trust for your Dad. The early illusory pictures had deeply imprinted in your mind relating both to your Dad and yourself.

You also unconsciously had a deeply abiding fear and resentment of women, that you could not permit yourself to admit or to openly, honestly express and work through. It is no wonder that you developed an inner longing for a non-threatening, self-satisfying relationship with another male who would not develop in your consciousness those frightening, overpowering, negative pictures of female domination and abuse.

The relief of that non-threatening sexual relationship with another male, accounts, in part, for the origin of the term, "gay." It becomes an escape from having to deal with those terrible emotional struggles of fear and unresolved anger and pain and imprisoning controls and responsibilities that bombarded your earliest impressionable consciousness.

However, the emotionally clouded information that you received in those earliest years was not accurate. The fact is you can unlearn what you negatively learned in that distorted climate. Within you are the inherently deeper spiritual resources that can bring healing and change through a total rethinking and recommitment of your personal sexual identity. Invalid thoughts, images and beliefs can be changed.

The idea is very scary, very troublesome and very challenging, but can be abundantly rewarding to your ultimate personal fulfillment and inner peace. Labels are created by past experiences that produce pictures of our minds. Labels that are dwelt upon and are constantly relived become beliefs. Whatever becomes programmed into your subconscious inevitably becomes action. That belief can feel like it is inherent.

I have utmost confidence in the universally originated spiritual resources available within each of us to make whatever changes we need and want to make along life's journey that will contribute to the love and intelligence of the God who created us.

Above all, I always have a deep and sustaining love and confidence in you, my son.

Lovingly, Dad

This letter is terribly sad for me on so many levels. While I agree with much of Dad's philosophies and ideas, there is an element that he just simply cannot understand. Being gay is not about choice. Not for me. All of the childhood occurrences he mentioned may have determined other issues in my adult life, but not my sexuality.

Ultimately, Dad and I have come to a place where it's all okay as long as we don't talk about it. But I wish I could relieve him of the pain and guilt he carries.

Dad's interpretation also fails to reckon with two things: that the best friends I've had as an adult, the people I most trust, generally are women – and that in my life, he's hardly the first powerful man who has tried to define what "being a man" should mean for me.

After my parents' divorce in 1957, when I was all of four, my grandfather Andrew Martin told me point-blank that I was now the man of the house and was expected to take care of my mother – to be her strong arm of support, a model of gentility and courtliness in public and in private. My Auntie Blanche tells a story of an evening at Lawry's Restaurant in Los Angeles, a favorite family spot where she and Uncle Bert were having a quiet dinner when Mother and I arrived. As usual, I was dressed as Little Lord Fauntleroy – jacket, short pants, fluffy bow tie and all. When we were shown to our table I struggled with a chair, trying to seat my mother as does a gentleman for a lady. The problem was that the chair was half again my size.

But expectations were clear. I was to stand when a lady entered or exited a room. I was to always offer my arm up and down stairs, open the doors, help her with her wrap, pay the bill and do whatever else was necessary to protect her safety and dignity. These were the rules of our home. I was instructed in what now would be considered an old fashioned world of formal bows, firm manly handshakes and gestures of a generous host. By age six, I knew how to mix a decent martini, converse with adults about their families, careers and current events – and yet resume when necessary my place as a child, seen and not heard, speaking only when spoken to. A difficult balance to sort out at that age.

Like the other adult men in my world, Grandpa Martin had a vision for me that was specific and rigid. I'll never forget a phone call early the morning of my ninth birthday. "Money is the most important thing in the world, boy!" I was then treated to a lecture about the significance of financial security and yet another about my responsibility to take care of my mother. He told me he'd opened a bank account in my name and would match any funds I could save or earn. In and of itself, not a bad offer. The only thing missing was discernible affection and a birthday greeting that might have felt less like a business transaction.

And the messages continued. Mother's second husband Jay Mancini was a macho, old-world Sicilian with a short temper and a powerful fist. When they were married, I remember he took down the beautiful Harlequin painting that hung above my bed and replaced it with his prize archery set.

I was an artistic child. I loved to read, draw and paint. I loved listening to my mother's record collection and creating in my own room a place of beauty and serenity.

I had an art box that housed all my treasures and supplies, and spent most of my free hours engrossed in projects that emanated from that box, projects that allowed me to escape into a gentler world of my own creation. Jay couldn't bear my artistic endeavors. He constantly made fun of me and the threat of violence was always clear if I chose those activities over the more manly pursuits he mapped out for me. I will never forget the day I put everything in my art box neatly in order, closed it for the last time and stowed it safely under my bed. I never opened it again. Jay replaced it with a toolbox, which I opened regularly to feign interest in the things that would not subject me to his insults, or the back of his hand.

Not all the men in my young life were controlling in ways that were uncomfortable to me. Granny's second husband David Lytell Hutton – Gramp to me – was loving and kind and encouraged my artistic endeavors. He had himself been a vaudevillian headliner and was a voice teacher. I spent hours at his voice studio in the Pantages Theater in Hollywood, listening to him teach lessons behind the frosted glass office door. It was the best voice training I ever had. Gramp was always ready to take me to the park, buy me a hot dog, or explain the intricacies of Barber's "Adagio for Strings."

And then there was his Cadillac, a car you wouldn't so much park as dock. It was 27 feet long with a red leather interior and white fins that looked to my eyes like a giant stingray. With its accumulated scent of decades of sweet pipe tobacco, the car was somehow both comforting and slightly dangerous.

The effects of childhood polio meant that Gramp struggled to perform many simple maneuvers – chief among them, driving. To drive, this man whom I loved and trusted in all things would steer with his left hand, and use his right hand to lift his leg from the gas peddle to the brake and back again. Terrifying to think of it today – but I remember no accidents, near misses or problems, only the concern I felt. After all, "This is my Gramp, and he can do no wrong!" And yet every time we approached a stop sign, I'd hold my breath.

Gramp

Now that I'm old enough to be a grandfather, I wonder how the inconsistencies of my life read to those I love and those who trust me. I hope the confidence outweighs the uncertainties. But all in all, I'd give anything to be back in that big old white barge that smelled like burning cherry trees, putting my life in his hands one more time. They were big, safe, strong, loving hands.

Gramp always walked with a cane or on crutches, but I never heard him complain. Raised in the pre-civil rights era South, he was a racially prejudiced man who stationed a black-faced "lawn jockey" by his front door, but to those he loved, including Granny and me, he was fair and kind. Toward the end of his life, he was bedridden for a number of years. But there was still wisdom and advice, stories to be told; still a seeking of spirit and redemption with hours poring over his Bible. Because brandy often was his solace, the words were sometimes slurred, but still a young man's inspiration.

Shortly after Mother's marriage failed, my Grandfather Martin placed me in military school, convinced it would toughen me up and "make a man" of me. It was one of the most painful parts of my childhood. The truth is, I *was* fat and soft. After a brief stint in the hospital for a bleeding ulcer, I'd been put on a diet of milk, cottage cheese, ice cream, puddings and foods thought to help my stomach. The result was a weight gain that surpassed the "Husky Boys" line of clothes. Carlsbad Military Academy had no uniform to fit me, so they had to special order one. It arrived in a different dye lot from the standard uniforms. I remember all too well the taunting of the other cadets: "There goes Nease, in the *special* uniform." It wasn't bad enough that I was probably the worst athlete on the grounds and couldn't make it around the track without losing my lunch, or that I had no interest in guns or the strict military regimens. To this day, I hate wearing anything green and can't bear the word "husky" whether it refers to someone's build or when my vocal chords are tired.

When at last I went to live with Dad and Jean, Dad did a really smart thing. Wanting his son to build a strong and healthy body, he went to the swim coach at Covina High School, explaining that I'd just come to live with him and imploring him to put me on the swim team. I persisted for three years and don't remember winning a race the whole time. So while the experience was good for my body, it was crushing to my ego. Mom, Dad, Cindy and Carolyn came to the meets to cheer me on, but I was hopeless. It was, however, a chance to build self-discipline, and a chance to recognize that I could face my fears. It also helped transform my body: In those three years, I went from 4'11" and 190 pounds to 6'1" and 165 pounds. It also gave me camaraderie with guys my own age I'd never known. I learned that I was more valuable than my fears and insecurities.

The older I get and the more I reflect, the more I credit Dad, in my youth, with giving me stability without strings. The four years after my folks were divorced when I lived with Dad, Joan, Sharon and Dad's stepmother Mamie (until I went to live with Mother halfway through third grade), and then another four years when

I lived with Dad and Jean, Cindy and Carolyn: These were the happiest years of my childhood. They were, in fact, the only years I was allowed to be a child.

Whatever uncertainties or distance our correspondence across the years created, whatever inner turmoil Dad's declarations caused, I know his intentions were loving. He wanted what he believed was best for his son. And God knows, I wanted to be a strong man, a leading man, on campus, in our family and the world. But most of the messages I received during those years were that I was not okay, not good enough, on the wrong track and not doing the right things. I was interested in pursuits that were not appropriate. The men in my life were defining me in ways that seemed to me not only limited, but much against my nature. Nonetheless, I determined to become the kind of man that was expected.

As an adult, that carried through into my career. I tried on stage to affect what I thought a manly stride and posture should be. Consequently, my early performances did not ring true. I was a caricature, projecting "leading-man-itus" rather than just being what I already was: an attractive, healthy young man who played a part, rather than playing my idea of what I should be. It seems my whole life has been about what it means to be a leading man, on stage and off.

I've come to realize that we are all studies in contrasts; grounded in diversity, mixed messages, trying to synthesize the disparate parts of our beings and balancing them with the expectations of others. To the degree that we embrace the diversity within our hearts and minds, as opposed to ignoring or denying the seemingly opposing parts of ourselves, I believe we can become fully-integrated human beings. Our humanity transcends our diversity of expression.

Whoever said: ***"What we resist, persists ..."*** got it right.

I may not be the son of my father's dreams – but in many ways, he has been the father of mine. For no matter the challenges, no matter the horrific circumstances in which he found himself, his quality of spirit has lifted him above and allowed him to go on, to re-invent himself.

His challenge to me to look deeply into what I believe was the inspiration for *From the Parsonage to Broadway,* a one-man show I performed in churches, speaking and singing about being gay within the church. Through all my searching I have not emerged where Dad might have hoped. But his admonitions made me strong in my convictions and my beliefs. In many ways, the apple did not fall so far from the tree. Just as my dad (and two generations of preachers before him) sought to inspire, inform and transform, in my own way, so have I.

When my sister Joan (his first born and favorite) died in 2004, I watched him navigate those waters with incredible grace and style despite the heartbreaking reality. After all the chaos of his life with my mother, he triumphed and re-invented himself, again. He kept moving forward, kept believing, kept striving, kept seeking the best in himself and in others. This is the man I see.

My dad once told me that the five most important words you can say to someone is "I am proud of you." He has not been able to say those words to me since 1980, until last year. But he does love me, even if it's in spite of rather than because of some parts of who I am. So though I no longer look for agreement, we have authenticity. In that, we are one. Of that, and him, I am proud.

Dad & Me – Today

"There's a thank you, you can give life, when you live life all the way..."
–Auntie Mame
Angela Lansbury, Jane Connell and me

I KNELT DOWN

"You're my best girl, and nothing you do is wrong ..."
Jerry Herman, MAME

I knelt down next to Angela Lansbury. She took my face in her hand and looked at me as if we were old friends. My fears melted away and my body stopped trembling. My heart was full, my dreams coming true. I sang one simple chorus of "My Best Girl" into those beautiful, owlish eyes I'd seen so many times on the big screen. Much as I wanted the job, that moment was worth all the years of work and auditions. This one felt right.

All eyes in the room were turned in my direction: the producer and his entourage, the casting director and his assistant, the musical director and his associate conductor, the choreographer, the stage manager, the composer and his assistant, Miss Lansbury's assistant, Clark Bason, and even her husband. It seemed as if an entire army had casting approval, and this was my moment.

My pulse was racing and I'm sure I was drenched. This was my fourth callback for a role I wanted desperately: the grown-up nephew Patrick to Miss Lansbury's *Mame* in a revival of that storied musical. As I sang to her, it was one of those magic moments where time stood still. When I looked at her, everything else faded away: In that moment, she *was* my Auntie Mame. Later, I would learn that's just who she is: a consummate professional who is always kind and giving, generous of spirit on stage and off, and every inch a great lady.

I left that audition hopeful and went to the pay phone to call my agent. After meeting a friend for lunch at Joe Allen's, I walked by Charley O's restaurant in Schubert Alley where Miss Lansbury and Jerry Herman were walking in. They called me over and told me I had the job. I don't remember what I did or said in that moment, though I'm sure hugging was involved. I do remember, about 30 seconds later, running into the middle of Times Square, into the triangle that separates Broadway and 7th Avenue and shouting at the top of my lungs. Kind of like Mary Tyler Moore to the background of her TV sitcom's theme song, "We're 'gonna make if after all ..." minus tossing the hat. I must have made quite a spectacle of myself because just across the street was Krista Newman and her then-husband Scott Bakula. They came running over to see if I was all right. I'd just finished doing *South Pacific* with John Raitt with Krista playing Nellie Forbush, the previous summer. And I'm sorry to say I don't think I'd shown that kind of enthusiasm as Lt. Cable in all the performances put together. I was delirious. I'm sure they thought I was quite mad.

Rehearsals were some time off, and I was both concretizing and cleaning houses. I'll never forget singing on the stage of Carnegie Hall on a Saturday night and on Monday morning I was cleaning someone else's toilet. I was constantly doing some hideous part-time job to fill in the gaps.

The contracts were signed, the script and score arrived, costume fittings began, and finally the first day of rehearsal. I was completely overwhelmed to be playing opposite so many actors who had been in the original *Mame* cast and were formidable personalities each in their own right: Jane Connell, Willard Waterman, Anne Francine, Louise Fletcher, John Becher, Barbara Lange. And across the room I spotted a dancer I'd never seen before. I knew instantly that I was in trouble.

Rehearsals were arduous but joyful. I learned so much by just watching people who were so confident in their craft. Though I had been working in and around New York and Los Angeles steadily since I graduated from college, this was a different league. There was a formula already created in this revival, almost a recreation. Everyone from the director to Miss Lansbury knew exactly what they wanted.

Jerry Herman was incredibly nice and wonderfully supportive. He was thrilled when Jim Coleman suggested we take "My Best Girl" up a key higher for me; and when the costume for one of my scenes wasn't right, he personally went to bat and paid for me to have a different blazer.

The dancer was still stealing more of my focus than I was willing to admit. I was doing my best to avoid contact and not pursue anyone with whom I was working. But I fall in love with talent; and the strength, style, and shear beauty of this man took my breath away. Finally, one day he was injured in rehearsal and was taken to a doctor. I called him that evening at home to see (innocently?) if he was okay. He said yes, and that I was exactly the person he'd hoped to hear from. I was a goner.

Rehearsals continued. We were to open at the Philadelphia Academy of Music, then do a 17-week tour before coming back into New York in the fall. Opening night in Philadelphia was, of course, thrilling and terrifying. I especially remember two things about that night. During a quick change I was in an alcove with Willard Waterman, whom I'd heard as the voice of "Tony the Tiger" and in so many films that just his voice felt like an old friend. As I frantically made my change, he said, "Remember to enjoy this moment. You are just beginning, and for me, this is a last hurrah." I felt so humbled and grateful for his wisdom.

And I really did take in the moment. It was thrilling to hear the audience responses and to see Miss Lansbury kicking her legs higher than all the chorus girls in the "Mame" number. Since I was playing "Older Patrick" and was in only the second act, I had lots of time to stand in the wings and watch. What a gift and lesson in true craftsmanship. And then there was the dancer. Since I don't dance a step, I'm in awe of what dancers are able to do and admire their discipline and the magic they create. This dancer, David, and I had finally made our connection offstage, and so I was able to go the opening night with someone of whom I was deeply enamored. He said he really wanted to "go for it" together, and I was ready for success on stage and off. What a great way to begin a new adventure: a national tour with Angela Lansbury and a new beau.

We opened to mixed reviews. Despite a backstage speech from our producer saying he was 100% behind us and we would ride it out, David and I found a crew loading up the trucks when we arrived at the theater the next day for the matinee. The production was moving back to New York, in the middle of summer with no advance and no publicity.

We opened at the Gershwin a couple of weeks later. David confessed that he had some "unfinished business" with someone he'd been seeing in New York. But as a token of something to come (and having sublet his apartment for the tour), he left his bright red trunk in my apartment. And so the opening night in New York was bittersweet. Again, reviews were mixed and though I was thrilled to be opening on Broadway with one of my dearest friends, I went home alone.

We struggled along with small houses, but I'll never forget everyone's pitching in putting up posters and giving away "two for one" tickets. For several days, Miss Angela's husband, Peter, drove several of us up and down Park Avenue, The Avenue of the Americas and Madison Avenue to many large corporations handing out discount tickets. By the end of the summer we were beginning to get a great response and the theater was filling.

I never knew what it really meant to "stop a show" until I worked with Miss Lansbury. Every performance when she made her entrance at the top of the stairs with the bugle, the explosion of adoration from the audience was like a wave immersing us all. Every performance, the "Mame" number stopped the show, as did "Bosom Buddies."

I was sharing a dressing room with Sab Shimono, the original Ito, on the second floor of the theater, stage right. The applause for "Bosom Buddies" lasted so long that I could wait until the song ended, get up, put on my jacket, go downstairs, cross all the dressing rooms leading to stage right, cross over and behind the huge expanse, and be there in plenty of time to make my entrance stage left. Unbelievable.

The red trunk finally took its toll. After three months of futile hopes and denial, I finally left David's trunk under his dressing table one night before the show. I began avoiding him as much as possible, taking different backstage paths during scenes where we'd formerly met for a quick hug or word. I was really heartbroken, I think much more than he knew. Perhaps the struggle of the show drove up the intensity of my feelings; I felt quite literally "left in the wings" waiting.

The show, on the other hand, was a continual joy and I was getting professional attention I'd never known before. Suddenly I was being noticed and talked about. I knew what Marilyn Cooper had meant when, accepting a Tony Award, she said, "I'm a poker player, and if you stay at the table long enough, you're bound to come up with a winning hand!" That's how it felt, after the previous years of struggling and near misses.

Sadly, we didn't run long. The "closing notices" had been put up pretty much every week backstage … then taken down. Finally, there weren't any for a couple of weeks and we were all hopeful that the crisis had passed. But the next week, I was watching our ad on the television and "FINAL WEEK" was flashing across the screen. That's how we all found out. Charming.

That night, Miss Lansbury called a company meeting backstage before we began. She was obviously devastated as were we all. But there were no harsh words spoken. In fact, she thanked us all and encouraged us to hold our heads high and go out with style and dignity. And she led the way. In fact, it was she who gave us a closing night party, with gifts for all.

The last few nights we all stood in the wings watching as much as we could. For her curtain call, Angela wore a white gown trimmed in white fur at the neck, sleeves and to the floor. It sparkled and flowed as she bowed like the theatrical royalty that she is.

On the final night, she barely got through her duet of "My Best Girl" with the Younger Patrick played by Roshi Handewerger. We were all so proud of him when he finished the phrase with her and stood up and offered a strong arm to escort her off stage. It is the one of the sweetest moments I remember. Also that night in the Mame number, each of the men in the company went down one at a time on one knee as Angela walked by, handing her a red rose. I was never so proud to be a part of such a magnificent group of people as I was on that night.

In the midst of the heart-breaking circumstances of closing *Mame*, Miss Lansbury had encouraged us to take the high road, to choose dignity over bitterness; though sometimes despite what is going on in our personal worlds, it is indeed a difficult task to be courageous behind the footlights as we challenge, provoke and entertain. But it is our ability on stage, which allows us the privilege to cut through the debris of a challenging time in our history.

In the aftermath of 9/11, in a letter to her colleagues, my friend Suzanne Ishee wisely wrote: "… *to depict the vagaries of human nature and in so doing, to enlighten and provoke heightened thinking and awareness, we have been granted the opportunity to tell stories that resonate directly to the crisis with which we and our audiences must now grapple. If, as actors, we do so with the honesty and commitment that honor our profession, we are given the forum and charged with the raising the consciousness of humanity. We do so, show by show, patron by patron.*"

I believe it is incumbent upon us to raise the bar, rather than pander to the lowest possible common denominator to affect change for the greater good as we entertain. This is the blessing of working with professionals like Miss Lansbury, whose humanity outshines their names in lights. This is the chance to "dream the impossible dream."

There truly are "no people like show people …" The magic I felt the first time I knelt by her side in that audition has carried through the past 20-plus years. For me, there has never been a moment on stage to equal that. Ever.

Theater Royalty
Miss Angela Lansbury

Me as Older Patrick

A family...at last
Dad, Mom (Jean) and Me

DELIGHTFULLY WICKED AND NOT-SO-STEP

"We are family…"
– Sister Sledge

*S*tep. I don't like that word. With it automatically comes a separation, a barrier. And though my life had been defined with many step-parents and step-grandparents (it was a much-married family), it always felt awkward. I always thought stepmothers and stepsisters were supposed to be "wicked." Not mine. Well, maybe the girls just a bit … but in a delicious way, not like in fairy tales.

It began at Granny's house. Always a place of refuge and love; always a place where I could pretty much do whatever I wanted. On this particular afternoon I was out by the pool on the bougainvillea-draped patio, with an art project spread out before me. It was a rare treat in those days: In my mother's home, such projects were not allowed, under an edict from her brutal and terribly strict second husband Jay. When they were happy, I was ordered to be happy with them. When they were fighting (which was most of the time), I'd get on my bike and go to Granny's.

And so Riverside Drive between Glendale and Burbank became my personal bike path to less volatile days and sweeter dreams. Here, my love for the arts was nourished rather than derided. Here I was happy. This was one of those days.

The phone rang at Thornwall-6578. Granny answered it in her office, and a few minutes later, I was summoned. It was a surprise! I ran through the den and grabbed the phone in the hall. Granny's bedroom door was closed, but I sensed her listening to my side of the conversation.

It was Dad. He had good news. He had just married Jean.

This really came as no surprise. My visitation weekends with him had been increasingly populated by Jean and her daughters Cindy and Carolyn. I had known them since I was born, and lately we'd all spent time together on my dad's boat called "The Mamie" after his (step)mother.

After the call, I got off the phone and cried. I was happy my dad was happy, and I liked Jean and her daughters. But the reality of his having another family scared me. At 12, I'd already spent most of my childhood on the road between Mother and Dad, Mother and Jay's family, Mother and Granny, Mother and Grandpa Martin and Mary, Mother and Mummy-Pat and Poppy, Mother and Auntie Ann, Mother and Auntie Blanche, visits to Joan, time away with my governess, military school, Boy Scout camps and several grammar schools.

In 1968, after six years in the custody of Mother, I wanted (and needed) to be with my Dad. I was tired of Mother's and Jay's abuse, and confused by mother's mother – who was well-intentioned but over-indulgent – and mother's father, who was verbally abusive.

I rode my bike to the Glendale Police Station, took off my shirt, showed them my bruises and asked them to help me get to my dad. Their response was to call my mother. When she came to pick me up, she gave an Academy Award winning performance. When she got me home, I was cruelly punished.

The next few days I was despondent and my homeroom and science teacher, Mr. Snyder, noticed. When he kept me after class one day, I blurted out the whole story. He called my father. A short time later, when I went to visit Dad for Father's Day, he picked me up and we went directly to his attorney's office. Bill Walk was a very kind man and listened to me as I told him my story. We signed papers asking the court to grant Dad custody; then Dad, Jean, Cindy, Carolyn and I high-tailed it out to Palm Springs where we "hid out" until Mother was served with the summons and to wait for the court date, set for 10 days later.

It was agreed, because of my age, that there would be arbitration rather than a hearing. I think in her heart of hearts, Mother knew what would come to light if this were to become as public as her and Dad's divorce, or the custody battle between her parents over her (when she was, ironically, exactly the same age I was, then). She had just opened Valley National Bank with Casey Stengel and didn't want any adverse publicity in her rising banking career. Too many of our family "secrets" had been front page news and the reason for gossip.

So on that afternoon, there was Mr. Walk, Dad, me; Mother, her attorney, her father and her half-brother (who had never shown the least interest in me, but gathered for Mother's moral support) and in an effort to intimidate at least me, if not Dad. Mother, of course was dressed to the nines, and my grandfather blustered into the room in his best "president of the corporation" mode.

Mr. Walk asked me to speak first. I don't remember what I said except that I wanted to go live with my Dad. Dad made a brief statement. We had an affidavit from Granny (Mother's mother) in support of Dad. Mother was unusually subdued; at one point she mouthed the words to me "I love you." I thought my heart would break. Even though I knew this was the right thing to do, I did love her and believed that in her own way, she loved me. It's just that there were two Mothers in one body, and the one who made me do the housework, make the meals and then tolerate her and her huband's verbal and physical abuse did not match up with the beautiful woman sitting in the attorney's office.

Grandpa Martin strutted and posed, said all manner of terrible things about my father and finally shouted, "As sure as we're sitting here, I'll be the one to have to put this boy through college." I remember speaking up to him for the first time in my life and said "I'd rather starve than ask you for ANYTHING!" Then I burst into tears. At that point, Mr. Walk brought things to a close and Mother reluctantly signed the papers. It helped that Joan and Sharon, many years earlier, had chosen to live with Dad as well.

A few days later, Dad drove me to Mother's home to collect some of my things, but she was unexpectedly there during business hours and wouldn't unlock the door. So, we returned to Dad and Jean's house …my new home, where Cindy and Carolyn took great delight in going through the clothes I did have with me. I remember fancy clothes flying as they threw out my blazers, ties, patent leather shoes and the accoutrements of a more formal lifestyle. We then went to the mall and bought Levis, tennis shoes, T-shirts and a bomber jacket for me. Oh, and a pair of Speedos. I was soon to find out why.

We had already formed a quick bond. We did not use the word "step," and in short order, Cindy and Carolyn were just my sisters, and Jean was Mom. Dad insisted I call her Mom, to honor her as his partner. It also established an immediate family structure, something I'd never known before. And it wasn't difficult. I loved Jean, and how happy she made my Dad. She was nice to me. Her parents made me feel like I was a part of their family. And she was a great cook.

One day near the end of summer, Mother and Jay arrived at Dad's house unannounced and uninvited. Mother's Lincoln was packed with my things. I remember being too scared to walk out to the front door, but Dad and I went together and retrieved my worldly possessions. When they drove away, it was a moment of very mixed emotion – but mostly, relief.

I did not see my Mother again for more than three years. I couldn't. I had too much healing to do. And like most teenagers, I was busy immersing myself in high school. Cindy, Carolyn and I were becoming fast friends and co-conspirators. Dad was teaching, back at school himself, earning another degree; Mom was working and I was experiencing a normal, family life for the first time.

Living with Mother, I had very few social skills outside of the world of rather sophisticated elders – so I embraced the opportunity to be a kid with relish. Again, Cindy and Carolyn were wonderful to me. Cindy was an ace student (something to which I'd never really aspired). Carolyn was hysterical, a wonderfully "bad" influence with the most infectious laugh.

They both took me on as a project, and gave me a crash course in being a normal guy. We did predictable high school stuff: football games, cruising the main boulevard in town. We'd go to the beach and swim (and attempt to surf), though it was the nachos at Huntington Beach I remember best. But the best part was, they really seemed to like me. To this day, I don't think I've ever laughed as hard as we did around the dinner table.

We'd gather for "family meetings," and for at least the first year, I was inevitably the topic of discussion over some inappropriate behavior. I was really trying, but I'd had no models for normalcy. Subtly, the focus shifted as my behavior improved, and as Carolyn drew more and more attention once she started dating – what a relief! She'd get us all laughing and I was off the hook. Cindy remained the good girl but was a party to the one thing for which we all consistently got into trouble: watching the Soaps. Every night after work, Mom or Dad would come home and see if the TV was warm. "All My Children" was our addiction.

I was finally outgrowing both my baby fat and my deep distrust for people, and beginning to enjoy life. I was not beaten. I was not ignored or shuttled off. I was loved and supported. These were four of the happiest years of my life. And I will always be grateful to the entire Nease tribe and our extended school and church community for finally giving me a look at what a happy, stable life could be.

We got involved at the Presbyterian Church in our community, I, probably more than the girls. I loved singing in the choir and the folk group there, and became involved in the Youth for Christ organization. Dad and Jean took me to a talent competition somewhere in the San Gabriel Valley. Scared to death, I sang "I Believe" – and I won. Then I won the regionals, and then the state competition – at 15, I was the youngest competitor ever to win at that level. Later that year, on the bus to Winona Lake, Indiana, for the national competition, I was miserably sick with a cold. I came in third place, but it was an amazing trip. And on one of our stopovers a bunch of us went to see the Barbra Streisand movie *Funny Girl.* I'd always loved musical theater, but that film affected me profoundly. Set against the competition in which I'd just sung, hearing her sing "I'm the Greatest Star" and "Don't Rain on My Parade" gave me a different sense of my destiny – and yet another clue to whom I was.

Transformation: Cindy & Me
In three years I went from short and fat to tall and thin.
Cindy just got prettier.

After the competition was over, I was invited to spend the rest of the summer in Ohio with an aunt and uncle on my Dad's side of the family. They had a large home on a pond, and three sons (one of whom was a swimmer – like me, only good). I'd never been away on my own this long and jumped at the chance. Floyd, the oldest son, was a bit of a rebel – smart, cool and everything I was afraid to be. He laughed at my calling myself a Young Republican (as do I, recalling it today). It was the first time I ever remember being really free. Not quite a man. Not quite a boy.

I returned to Los Angeles with a whole new perspective, more determined than ever to be my own person. I dropped the Young Republicans. I embraced swimming with new relish. I was determined to be "one of the guys." I still couldn't reconcile my lack of desire for a girlfriend. But I'll never forget my first kiss with Diane Schell. It was on a hayride. Not very good (on my part) but I was going to make it happen come hell or high water! Because something very significant had just happened.

My sisters Joan and Sharon were now grown and married. My memories of them, of living with them as a small boy, were childhood memories, just a blur. Joan was married and having children of her own, and though I saw her once in a while, she was not in those years a daily part of my world. Sharon had long since been married, lived in Northern California, and then moved to Germany. She'd been gone for what seemed like an eternity and when she came home unexpectedly, I knew something very bad had happened. It was only discussed in whispers. But I knew that it was resonating in my life, too. It terrified me. Sharon's husband was no longer with her but with someone else. Someone male.

What had happened with Sharon's husband terrified me, struck me as it struck no one else in the family – because this very bad truth about her husband, I knew, was also about me. I always had known, on some level. I just couldn't admit it. And now amidst this heartbreak and pain in Sharon's life, I buried it even deeper inside. But I knew. I knew.

What I did not know or yet understand was two things. First, I was not bad and wrong for being gay. I did not choose it any more than I chose the color of my hair. God created all of me. The second thing was that the spiritual part of my being was not the same thing as being Born Again Christian. It was too deeply ingrained in my history and that of my family. It was a lesson yet to be learned.

Then, out of the blue, the unthinkable happened. Dad had a heart attack. I was terrified, both at the thought of losing my Dad and at the prospect of having to go back to live with my mother. But my worries were unfounded; Dad recovered. One day during his convalescence, one of Jean's brothers, Allen, took me out to lunch. He reassured me that Dad would be all right, stated flatly that my new family would want me even if Dad were not around – and told me that, anyway, I was old enough to make my own decisions, legally. Since he was a California Highway Patrolman, I believed him. I will always remember his kindness that day.

At the end of my junior year, I finally stopped swimming in order to be in the choir. My school was doing *Annie Get Your Gun* that year, and though being in choir was suspect, I wanted to do the lead in that musical. And I did. My first leading lady was Carla Deal, a vivacious redhead with a great voice and spunk to match the part. I remember rehearsing long and hard, and finally we opened at the theater of the local junior college.

I think I was pretty good; at 17, I had most of the voice I have now, although I looked about 12. In any case, it was my first real triumph in my new life. We ran for four performances. I'll never forget closing night whooping it up and running out the stage door ready to party. And out of the corner of my eye, I saw Mother and Jay walking toward their car. I guess Granny must have told her about the show. I ran and caught up with them. I think it was a shock for all of us. It had been three years, and I had changed dramatically, from short and pudgy to tall, lean and still growing. It was an emotional, uncertain reunion, and the beginning of building back some semblance of a relationship. Over the next couple of years Jay was still in and out of the picture, but visits with Mother (though sporadic) increased.

Like most teenagers, I was too self-involved to make too much of an effort, and probably was not ready anyway. My senior year was great. I had finally grown into my body, and thanks to Cindy's popularity, was being accepted. I was on the yearbook staff and in, if not the most envied guy's service club … the #2 club. But I I didn't care – at least I got the coveted jacket. I was on the student council and because of my success with *Annie Get Your Gun*, was suddenly a big guy on campus, at least in my mind. Then it happened: Julie Lyons (only THE most popular girl in school) asked me to be her escort at the Homecoming half time. And she was queen! That cinched it. I was in.

To pick up spending money, I was working at Baskin-Robbins and, because Jean was the organist at the local Episcopal church, I began to sing at weddings and funerals in the community. At funerals, the screen behind which the vocalist stood was directly behind the casket: surreal. But at $25 per song, it was big money in 1970. I'd have swung from the chandeliers singing for those "big bucks."

That year, a vocal group called The Spurrlows came to my high school for an assembly. It was thrilling. They stayed and the next evening did a more religious concert. I wanted to be one of them. I wanted to travel and sing. I auditioned for Kirk Lytell, the lead singer. He encouraged me to go to their audition camp that summer. I became obsessed with being in that group. As I think about it now, it was a rather daring thing for me to do in 1970, and perhaps an even braver thing for Dad and Jean to contemplate. But I traveled to Troy, Michigan and attended a four-day audition camp. I did not get into the Spurrlows. But there was another group within the organization called The Re'Generation. Their director and arranger, Derric Johnson, offered me a spot in his group. At 17, I was by far the youngest in The Re'Generation. But it was a wonderful environment for me in terms of a way to leave home. I was safe, well protected, on a mission, learning my craft and got $21 per week in "toothpaste money."

And so, the morning after graduation and my Senior All Night Party, Cindy and one of my best swimming buddies, Rob James, drove me to El Centro, California, where I would spend the next few weeks of my life preparing for the following year.

When I said goodbye to Dad, Jean and my not-so-step-sisters, it never occurred to me that things might not always be the same between us. I was naïve. Our lives would eventually take us down different paths, and different ideologies. But I will always be grateful for the time we had, and the first real family I could remember.

In 2006, Carolyn died. The years between our loving family times in Covina and her death were filled with difficult times and much tragedy for her. Carolyn married just out of high school and shortly thereafter gave birth to a beautiful daughter, Tracy Lynette. Carolyn's husband was in the Army and stationed in Germany at the time of Tracy's birth. It was not long before we learned this beautiful child was hydro-cephalic. Her little body could barely support her head; she never learned to walk or was able to play with others. Tracy's world consisted of constant trips and extended stays at the Children's Hospital in Los Angeles. There were countless hours in hospital corridors, procedures and hours spent amongst the family, rallying around Carolyn and Tracy.

I keep on my nightstand a small photo of this angel sent to us for too short a time. I remember singing to her and playing a game she liked identifying "eyes, ears, mouth, chinny-chin-chin ..." The expertise of the doctors, the consistent love of her mother and the support of her family was not enough to keep her with us. When we buried Tracy in 1975, I think we buried a piece of Carolyn as well.

The years went by and Carolyn and her husband Wayne were blessed with another child – a son, Daniel Wayne Murphy. From the beginning, Danny was a fine boy and good son. He was athletic and is still built like a linebacker. He has his mother's wit and his father's steadfast devotion to family. Daniel became a police officer in Southern California while completing his education. During that time his father, Wayne succumbed to cancer and once again we buried another part of Carolyn with him. Daniel stood by and took masterful care of his mom in what became a complicated set of medical challenges that ultimately and unexpectedly ended her life with us.

As a performer I've learned that both words and music have vast power, but they also remind me about being mute in the face of some moments. The death of a loved one – especially a Carolyn – teaches me how inarticulate I can be. I wish I knew language to truly convey comfort.

What makes a sister? Is it genetics? A common history? A meeting of minds and spirits? All of these, I think. Carolyn, though a lifelong acquaintance, became my sister when my father was wise enough to choose her mother as his bride in 1964. She became my friend increasingly across the years, demonstrating that you can love someone completely without complete understanding. Carolyn was always a great conspirator. She taught me how to sneak out of the house. She taught me to drive a stick shift on Kellogg Hill and never to wear tassels on my shoes.

While most girls her age were defined by the conventions of their schools, communities, family values and adolescent pressure – Carolyn was just Carolyn. Funny, smart, effervescent, rebellious, devilishly charming; able to incite a small riot at family dinners and leave us weak with laughter, totally disarmed by her outrageous honest assessments of that which most people would try to hide. I remember a neighbor commenting to another, "What goes on in the Nease household? Nothing can be that funny!"

Carolyn taught us all how to play. During our high school years, I remember riding in the back seat of her Mercury sedan, with her pushing my head down so I couldn't be seen when a cute boy would drive by. I spent a great deal of time on the floor of that back seat. I remember days at Huntington Beach where I would swim and she would pose for the life guards … and always, the quest for the perfect burrito, never fully realized.

Carolyn, of us all, was the rebel. She simply forged her way on her own terms. As we grew and changed, I was the most distant and more foreign to her world. And yet Carolyn never judged me. She just loved me for all of who I was. She demonstrated that to be a good friend, you must leave someone with all of their freedom intact.

Carolyn and her family made many trips to be a part of my world, in New York, Toronto, Vancouver and Denver. She also freely included me in hers. She knew on a primal level that we all belonged to each other and claimed the kinship of her family. It's that quality of spirit, of unconditional love amidst the uncertainties of life, that I miss so much (along with her enchiladas and lemon cake).

Somewhere in the Bible comes the counsel to rejoice with those who laugh and weep with those who mourn. It occurs to me that this is not so much an injunction, as something we all do naturally when we love. When I laughed with Carolyn we honored the best that is in us all, our kinship. And it is her laughter I will miss most of all. It rings in my heart today, and always shall.

Kahlil Gibran said: *"When you are sorrowful, look again in your heart, and you shall see the truth ... you are weeping for that which has been your delight."* I weep for that delight of my sister. I am grateful to have lived in the shadow of her heart.

Carolyn & Me…

Me with my first bible

JUST AS I AM

"Jesus loves me this I know, for the Bible tells me so. Little ones to Him belong. They are weak, but he is strong. Yes, Jesus loves me, the Bible tells me so…. Jesus loves the little children, all the children of the world. Red and yellow black and white, they are precious in his sight. Jesus loves the little children of the world."

– Anna B. Warner and David Rutherford McGuire

Nothing moves me more than the hymns of my childhood. As an adult, I question some of the words and their meaning, yet the strains of "In the Garden," "Amazing Grace," "Just As I Am," or "Balm In Gilead" can stir my heart and soul.

Growing up in my father's church, I grew up in a world of love … and a world of secrets. There was love in our family, love for and from the congregation and love for God. But there were also all those family secrets we kept from the congregation - and some secrets I dearly hoped I could keep from God.

This song I learned in my time with 'the Re'Generation' best describes some of my earliest years:

"I grew up in a parsonage and my Father preached the word. He taught the love of Jesus, and the people sometimes heard. They'd listen to the message, and often say 'AMEN!" But I was six and restless, and I loved the closing hymn … and when I think of Jesus, and how He suffered so … I think about His Father, who had to watch Him go. And now that I am older, a likeness I can see; of the love of my two Fathers, that they have had for me."

The older I get, the more questions I have, rather than answers to what God may or may not be, and specifically in regard to how I was raised to believe and that which most of the Judeo/Christian tradition imposes. My sisters never stepped inside a church again after they were on their own, nor have their children. I have taken classes in comparative religion, done a great deal of reading, investigated many denominations and philosophies. I have come to a belief that the divine is not something separate, but is within each of us.

The best little boy in the world

And so, my journey from the parsonage to Broadway, with a few stops in-between, has been for me a journey from religion to spirit. I still love singing in churches. It's so much a part of who I am, and how I was raised. But my journey to manhood has taken me down different roads philosophically.

When I was living with Dad as a small boy, it was in a parsonage. They say that PKs (preachers' kids) are the worst. I don't know how true that is. I think that my worst sins were probably yawning loudly at strategic moments of Dad's sermons, or penciling in all the Os in the church bulletin or the hymnal with my buddies while huddled in the back pew of the church. And I did like to sing parodies of hymns that would annoy my dad, like "The church's one foundation, is tax deductible!"

I got my start in music in the church, as do so many performers. I think my first solo was at about the age of four singing "The B-I-B-L-E, yes that's the book for me ..." I remember the opening hymn every Sunday was "All Hail the Power of Jesus Name, Let Angels Prostrate Fall." I didn't quite get it and sang, "All hail the power of Jesus name, let angels' prostates fall." Of course I had no idea what I was saying, but as soon as I was advised that it was the wrong thing to say, I loved doing it even more. Such naughtiness was about as bad as I got, ever mindful that I needed to be "the Best Little Boy in the World." I wanted God's love too much. I still wanted Dad's love too much.

Dad in his study at the church

My first conceptions of God sprang from the cover of the original cast recording of *My Fair Lady*. That cover bore a famous Al Hirshfeld drawing of George Bernard Shaw up in the clouds manipulating the marionette strings of Eliza Doolittle and Henry Higgins. I thought that's who God was. But then, I'd received such conflicting messages about God. What I did know early on was that God was a separate being from me. Way out there, somewhere. God was

definitely male – there was no question about the gender of God, in our household. He looked something like a cross between Santa Claus and Charlton Hes-
ton, but on a throne way up in the sky. And the scriptures characterized His
mood swings from loving to vengeful. I was hopelessly confused.

For as long as I can remember, I've been attracted to Buddhas – an affinity
not encouraged in my strict religious upbringing. I was five or six when, on a
shopping trip, I talked my Granny into buying me a little plastic, brightly-col-
ored Buddha about six inches high. I took it home and Dad wouldn't allow it. I
remember crying, not understanding and telling Granny about it, believing she
could fix anything.

I remember the conversation so clearly. She sat me down at the dining room
table with my drawing pad and a crayon. She drew a big circle, divided it into slices,
and said, "Think about this pie as religion. The Catholics are one piece, the Jewish people another, the Muslims, Episcopalians, Baptists, Nazarenes, Method-
ists, all pieces. You see, they are all paths to God. But not any one of them is the
whole pie. And the strength is in the seeking." *The strength is in the seeking*. She
explained it in a way that a small boy could understand, and that stays with me
to this day.

I decided I'd figure it out when I was an adult, because adults knew everything. We had fathers and Presidents who presented facades to their families
and the nation, that they knew it all. So I assumed that I too would understand
when I got older. You can imagine my shock when I realized we all make it up as
we go along.

There's another story I heard – true or not true, doesn't much matter – that
speaks to my personal spiritual journey. It begins with a father, mother and little
boy, very happy together – and even happier at the arrival of a new baby, a little
sister. From the time the child was brought home, the little boy kept begging
his parents to spend time alone with his little sister. They were very protective
and rather suspicious, but finally after weeks of his entreaties, they agreed. They
watched through the cracked nursery door as the boy went to the crib, gently
took his sister's tiny hand in his own small one, and made this quiet request:
"Sister, remind me about God. I'm beginning to forget."

I want to find the child in me again. I've unlearned too much.

I remember when I was about six or seven, I went to a revival, a community-
wide tent meeting that my father's church hosted. I was terrified. The visiting
evangelist was a "Hell-fire and brimstone" preacher whose words were meant

to browbeat people into confessing their sins in exchange for eternal salvation. Well, I didn't want to get left behind, so I went forward for the altar call, hoping to be revived. But the result was that later that evening I went home crying and screaming, "I'm going to Hell ... I'm going to Hell ... I'm a sinner." I had no idea why or even exactly what that was, but I knew on that night I was one and would "suffer the wages of death." (By now, of course, all manner of television evangelists have let me know why I categorically am bound for Hell. What a relief to be clear about it.)

As I tried growing up to distinguish between religion and spirit, while balancing my imagined demons, I constantly found myself drawn to the music and the spirit while resisting the religion. Any church that tells me it is the "only true way to God" sends me running the other direction. I got lots of messages from family, friends, teachers, the media and most upsettingly of all, from the church ... that I was not okay if I just showed up and told the truth about who I was. Gratefully, I now believe that God loves all the parts of me that He/She created, not just the ones with which the Moral Majority is comfortable.

I have gathered so much conflicting information about God and religion, from my earliest childhood memories, to the studying and reading I've done as an adult. As I've looked for spiritual meaning both outside and inside myself, I've tried many things. I tried motivational seminars, I tried therapy, I tried twelve-step programs. I've tried progressive, non-traditional churches with "inclusive language" – although when I hear "God the Mother of us all," though I believe it to be true, I still have trouble saying it. I've tried chanting, astronomy, astrology, numerology ... all the "ologies."

But there is a difference between faith and fact and what history documents and faith dictates; the truth, to me, remains uncertain. Countless books and theories about Jesus, God, the origins of the church and the veracity of what most of the modern world holds to be sacred are in conflict. Scholars have well established many historical facts that unhinge the rudiments upon which our spiritual culture is based.

To put it into a historical context, in the early days of Christianity, the people were largely uneducated and superstitious. Theirs was a verbal tradition. Most of the stories and words of Jesus were not actually transcribed for decades after his death. No one can be certain about their true origin nor who authored them.

I believe that the principles as set down through the life of Christ (as are those of Gandhi, Buddha, Socrates, Confucius and so many great men across the ages) are life's highest priorities. Those tenets are what I seek to pursue, though I fall short more often than not. So my choice is to look beyond the money changers in the temple – those evangelists who promise us a place in Heaven for a check. Do we really need a heavenly bribe or threat of damnation to behave decently?

It is difficult to believe that any human being has the capacity to put words around what God might be. But where I see God most clearly is in the eyes of those who love me. So that if indeed we are created in the image of God, that must be a magnificent reflection. When we choose to be, I believe we are the means by which Grace and Mercy flow. For instance, forgiveness. It has always been a stumbling block for me. I know I need it. I find myself constantly asking for it regularly from my friends and loved ones, and I count on those I love to forgive me. I was raised on all the axioms: "Forgive 70 times 7," "Turn the other cheek," "Forgive and forget." Who wants to forget, especially if it leaves you open to being hurt again? My choice is to forgive, and remember, and move on. As my dad told me many years ago: *"True compassion is the understanding of the lack of understanding."*

It is difficult for me to consistently access gratitude in the midst of uncertainty. But I've had too many examples in my darkest hours not to embrace it. I have learned the human manifestation of Grace through my friends and family as I have traveled down the road from the early days of AIDS/HIV when our lives were defined by hospice to today, where the concerns are dealing with the affordability of the life-saving treatments and their long-term side effects. But, these are problems of blessings.

Grace. Two specific incidents come to mind. The first involves one of my leading ladies in *Phantom*, Mary D'Arcy. During the dance sequence of the extravagant "Masquerade" scene, my nose started to bleed. Though I had been painstakingly careful about how I kissed my love interests on stage, and although Mary knew of my health status, I was still terrified when after the bleeding stopped and I had returned to the stage to finish the sequence. It came time for me to kiss her. I turned my face away and she whispered in my ear, "It's OK, you don't have to be afraid to kiss me." That's Grace.

The other was when I told my Uncle Bob and Aunt Betty that I was HIV-positive. First, they asked me how they should pray for me. My response was for peace of mind. They responded by telling me that should I ever need a place to go in case of illness and to be cared for, that I could come and stay with them. This, coming from devout Christians whose beliefs and perceptions could not be further from my own. Again, Grace.

As an adult, I finally found my church home at Riverside Cathedral in New York City and joined there in the mid-1980s. I became active in that church, because I believe that uncertainty and fear are both greater when you are not participating in a solution.

The minister at the time, William Sloane Coffin, was riveting, political, funny and inclusive. From him I learned that you must be able to laugh at what you hold sacred, and still hold it sacred. The work that church does, to me, is the best example I've seen of the church alive in the community: outreach programs that feed the poor, shelter the homeless and serve a host of other disenfranchised groups. Completely inclusive. But again, it was the music that really pulled my heartstrings and kept me attending year after year.

And so I keep going back, choosing to look beyond the well-intended structures with the knowledge that love, mercy and community are possible and that places like Riverside Church honor diversity and give me a spiritual home.

My musical director, Phil Hall, wrote a song I once had the privilege of singing at Norman Vincent Peale's Church, Marble Collegiate. The lyrics hold deep meaning for me:

"Father, so you call us all your children, regardless of our color creed or race? Is there something I could ever do or feel or be, that might cause me to live outside of Grace? Wanting to be whole is what I long for, putting angels in some demon's place. And while I'm not unwilling to confront what lies ahead, give me the strength to face what I must face. If the road to light seems filled with darkness; and still to this road you make your way. Hope Springs Eternal ... today.

"It's not benign perfection that I ask, child. Or mindless prayer offered thoughtlessly. It's not using the Bible to condemn or to conform. But using it to be all you can be. It's embracing one's humanity I ask for. It's helping one who seems to have lost their way. It's responding to one's needs with great compassion. It's faith in what you do as well as say."

One of my favorite hymns that has for the past couple of years played like a mantra in my head is "It Is Well With My Soul." It was written by a man named H.P. Spafford during a devastating time in his life. The story goes like this. He had put his wife and three daughters on a trans-Atlantic cruise. There was a shipwreck, and when his wife finally cabled him from London, it was simply two words ... "Saved alone." He took the next ship available, and asked the Captain to let him know when they got to the spot where his daughters had drowned. And as he sailed across their watery graves, he wrote out these words:

"When peace like a river surroundeth my way. When darkness like sea billows roll. Whatever my lot, thou hast taught me to say, it is well … it is well with my soul."

I don't think anything has taught me more about my soul than the discovery almost 25 years ago, that I am HIV-positive. On the day I received that diagnosis, I stopped trying to convince God to love me. Ironically, what I found in letting go of God is that God does not let go of me. When I am weak, God embraces me. When I walk the floors at night, God walks with me. When I am in tears at the loss of yet another friend, God cradles me.

On the difficult days, denial helps, but denial ends. Forgetfulness helps … a call from a friend helps me, a hug from someone I love, a stiff drink, a wonderful audience, but my forgetfulness ends. And what I am left with is something I cannot create, cannot fabricate, cannot innovate. It's something that my grandmother called Grace. It's not about being good or bad, right or wrong. It's about being loved, anyway.

When I was a kid, I heard a great deal about how I was supposed to love God. What I didn't truly know was how much God loves me. That was the lesson I needed to learn. That is what HIV has helped teach me. This hymn, "He Giveth More Grace", sings to our souls:

"He giveth more Grace when the burden grows greater. He sendeth more grace when your labors increase. To added affliction is added sweet mercy. To multiplied trials is multiplied peace."

It really does come down to the matter of faith. I have spent so much time looking at what is wrong with the church, I sometimes forget about faith, and that millions of people around the world depend on the church for guidance and solace. I must filter out that which is beyond reason. When one looks closely at the compassion and good works the church encourages and offers, it is miraculous.

Mother Theresa once said, "If we are to have any long lasting relationships with people or nations, we must learn to forgive lavishly." *Lavishly.*

That means the church, each other and most importantly, ourselves. It's not about facts, it is about feeling. Faith is what you see when your eyes are closed. When there is nothing left but God, that is when you find that God is all you need.

JUST THE SEMBLANCE OF A FACE

"Who am I anyway, am I my resume, that is a picture of a person I don't know ..."

– Marvin Hamlish

After my run in *The Phantom of the Opera*, I'd assumed I would be somewhat inured to physical deformity. But when the doctor held the mirror to my face and I saw the gaping hole in my nose, I immediately had two thoughts: I will never work again and no one will ever love me again. In the performance of the *Kopit/Yeston PHANTOM*, I had delivered this line: "Because I have no face. I have only the semblance of a face. No one should have to look at it." But no matter how solid my skill at performing that moment on stage, the reality of living it in my life was something quite different.

Due to facial wasting that had become increasingly visible, I had not really looked at my face for a couple of years. Oh, I looked at my hair when I combed it. I looked at my teeth when I flossed. I looked at my chin when I shaved. But I had not, really, looked at the entirety for a long, long time. The ravages of the medication had made me unrecognizable to myself and those who loved me; my appearance was making me self-conscious about auditions and, I was sure, costing me jobs. Then the 2002 diagnosis of basal cell carcinoma and the resulting laser surgery left my nose with a hole the size of a nickel and almost a half-inch at the deepest point. I was grateful the cancer was caught before it spread further – but I'd nearly exhausted my ability to be optimistic.

Anti-retroviral (ARV) drugs have been a godsend, with their ability to keep the virus from growing and replicating. But they come with their own side-effects, some of them vicious. I started using AZT, the first ARV approved for use in this country, in 1994. Over time, it left my feet riddled with neuropathy, damage that impairs nerves' ability to send pain and sensation impulses to the brain. At first, it was just a numbness and lack of sensation that sent me clumsily sprawling on more than one occasion. Then the alternate burning and coldness began along with the prickling "pins and needles." I devised ways to get around town that minimized walking, plotting each day which route would be shortest, least painful. Still, by the end of any given day I was limping – not the best look for a leading man whose onstage gait should be a self confident, easy stride.

The ARVs also cause lypodystrophy, which drains fat from some parts of the body and deposits fat in others. I developed a "buffalo hump" between my shoulders that rivaled any dowager's, a "protease paunch" in my lower abdomen, and a "horse collar" of fat pads around my neck that made me think of *Star Wars'* Jabba the Hut. Meanwhile, the fat vanished from places where I couldn't afford to lose it. My face was gaunt and hollow-cheeked; the flesh disappeared from my behind, making it virtually impossible to sit for any length of time without pain and eventually the bones breaking through.

And if I was looking less the leading man, thanks to the drugs, I was sounding less the leading man as well. ARVs can have a disastrous drying effect on the vocal cords. My vocal stamina and range were so affected that at times, it was almost impossible to sing what once was totally effortless. At other times, my voice served me as well as it ever did – but it's powerfully unnerving, facing a crowd of thousands at some event and wondering if the voice will be there when I need it.

And so life in my forties was unfolding. Skin cancer spots on my head, forehead and chest, thanks to heedless days of youth on the Southern California beaches. Two bouts of radiation to address incipient malignancies elsewhere. Medication-induced intermittent sexual dysfunction. The ever-present fear of needing a liver transplant, if my liver gave out after years of metabolizing these medications that were saving my life.

Through it all, I was walking a thin line. Long-term survivors of HIV can't just capriciously drop this drug and try that one, for fear of building resistance to the available drug families. So I find myself continually buying time, trying to fine-tune existing medication combinations until the next round of new-and-improved drugs are available and the next … and the next … and the next.

The financial costs of managing the disease have also been exorbitant. In addition to the cost of my regular medication (at one point over 140 pills a day, including supplements), there have been dozens of alternative treatments: acupuncture, guided meditation, electro-enhancement, massage, special diet, sessions with "healers," psychological help, spiritual gurus, and on and on. Insurance? You must be joking.

Through the uncertainties, it is clear that I am one of the lucky ones. I have seen people die of AIDS and I have seen people choose to live with HIV. Of course, genetics, medical care, multiple infections of different strains of the virus and when you contracted it all bear a part. But I'm convinced that the quality of human spirit plays a bigger part. In any case, I had just about reached the end of my ability to cope when it came time for my 50th birthday.

When I heard about a seminar on possible treatment for facial wasting, I was desperate to attend but terrified to go alone. My friend Phil Hall agreed to go along, to lend moral support plus another set of eyes and ears. We took a seat in a seminar room full of people who had faces – or lack thereof – like mine. The seminar presenter had barely begun when I started to weep. The photos she showed took my breath away: the "before" shots looking sadly familiar, but the "after" shots looking restored, healthy, whole.

This was the first hope I'd let myself feel in years. Would it really be possible to regain my face, my behind – my life as I'd known it? The seminar brochures suggested it might, as did testimonials from people who had been through the process, which involved injecting a permanent filler material into areas where muscle tissue had been lost, and removing excess tissue where it had deposited.

The brochures also told me I couldn't afford the treatments, since keeping myself fed, housed and medicated in Manhattan took every dime I made. But somehow I felt better just knowing help was out there – that someday, I might no longer look like a freak to myself or like a sick person to the rest of the world.

I didn't see Phil again until about eight weeks later, at a party at the home of my friend Linda Ellerbee. During those weeks, Phil had been busy: He and dear pals Sally Fisher and Scott Barnes had invited a few dozen of my friends to chip in on a 50th birthday surprise. And so that night at Linda's, they gave me the gift of beginning again: A stack of checks from friends all over the world, to pay for the reconstruction procedures. Someone read a long and beautiful toast that included these unforgettable words: "You have outlived every prediction, to our great joy." I just stood there, tears coursing down my sunken cheeks.

My "Before and After" photos that tell the story:

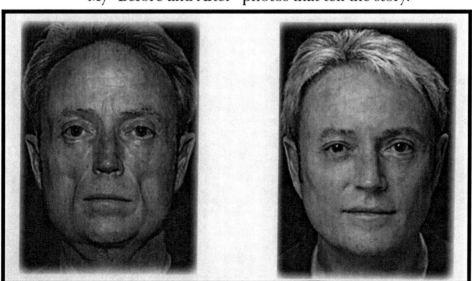

Out of need came restoration. Out of uncertainty came a community of loving support. I have always known I am rich in my friends. But this gift was so humbling, so overwhelming that to this day, I smile through tears to think of it.

To date, I've now had multiple sessions of facial reconstruction, plus several treatments to re-pad my derriere. The horse collar, hump and paunch all have been reduced through repeat procedures and, as tissue is re-deposited, all will have to be done again. But for now, my back is smooth, my belly flat, and my neck back to a normal shape. My feet will never be out of pain and I still mis-step frequently, because the neuropathy's damage is irreversible. But I am now able to sit, pain free – and, frankly, with a better behind than I had at 25!

Those of us infected with HIV have been known to jokingly call this virus "The Gift That Keeps On Giving." But really, that's true only for the fortunate ones among us. In the mid-'80s when I was diagnosed HIV-positive, it was a death sentence. Now, with the right treatment – and yes, some luck – HIV/AIDS is increasingly a manageable disease in the developed world. I have surely had my periods of depression and depletion: nights of fearful waking, and days of facing down some new threat. But who among us doesn't have those episodes? No one travels through this life without some challenges. Everyone is called to the test.

Even when life is tough, I find that I am tougher if I summon the best that is in me. I fall back on faith. I pray. Over and over, I empty myself to begin again – to hope again, to love again, to choose more life. I roll with all the medications, surgeries and treatments not just to keep the "semblance of a face" that show business requires. I do so to keep faith with everything and everyone that brought me this far; to honor optimism and friendship, resilience and reinvention. And I take inspiration from a lyric by my friend David Friedman:

"So open your hearts, open your minds,
no matter how you've tried and failed,
tomorrow you may turn and find that Help Is On the Way,
from places you don't know about today,
from friends you may not have met, yet believe me when I say,
I know, Help Is On the Way!"

Me today…

It may be only "the semblance of a face," but by the grace of God and with help from my family of friends, it is a face I am no longer ashamed to show.

SURVIVOR

*"Once I was afraid, I was petrified … Oh no not I,
I will survive"*

– Gloria Gaynor

As the years roll by, both the dynamics and the perception of the HIV/AIDS pandemic have changed. Particularly in the United States, many people, even in the gay community, have some sense that "it's over" or, at least, manageable. And so the attention wanes even though the illness rages: striking disproportionately in American among the poor, the disadvantaged, women and people of color; devastating Africa, India and spreading at alarming rates in Asia and elsewhere.

After all these years of living with HIV, I know something about its toll – the loss of friends, the loss of dignity. I understand the importance of hospice, the impossibility of medical bills, and the improbability of my being here today. Mostly, what I have learned is simply how to survive. I was told by a breast cancer survivor that the only definition of survival is: to survive.

I've spent much of my life on stage, where we measure time in terms of runs. When I played Raoul, the romantic lead in *The Phantom of the Opera*, my run lasted five years. When I first suspected that I was HIV-positive in 1983, I expected a run – that is, a lifespan – of two years, tops.

There is a phenomenon known as survivor's guilt. For some, it is easier to die from, than to live through. I stopped counting when the AIDS-related deaths among my friends hit 70. But when I think of them – Paul Penfield, Dennis Fox, Joseph del Ponte, Rob Eichberg, Jim Slemmons – and of how they just missed the window of the life-prolonging medications that finally became available, I do understand survivor's guilt. And I ask the self-indicting question: If they're gone, why am I still here?

There's a deadly serious consequence to long-term survival when it's the illness that has slipped out of the spotlight. Except for a little *frisson* of interest in summer 2006 marking the 25th anniversary of the first AIDS diagnoses, the public consciousness of HIV/AIDS has receded dramatically, and alarmingly.

Twenty years ago, AIDS awareness was growing with every panel added to the Quilt; it was a cohesive community, chiefly gay men and their celebrity friends. It was a floodlit cause. Now it's a fractured community at best; its newer recruits may have nothing more in common than the disease.

When I think of what responsibility comes with survival, my mission becomes much greater than just myself. If indefinite, generally-healthy survival is the new reality, then it's time for all of us – everyone who's HIV-positive, and everyone who knows someone who's HIV-positive – to reorient our thinking. If HIV-infected people are truly – remarkably – going to grow old, then we also need to grow in understanding. We need to come to terms with what it means to be HIV-positive and *not* dying – that it could be both the greatest gift pharmacopoeia can give us and the hardest thing we've ever done.

If there is to be any true AIDS advocacy – any band to champion the rights and needs of people with this illness – perhaps we long-term survivors must lead the quest to build it. A quarter century on, I am one of the old soldiers of this virulent war. We pushed ahead as comrades, once, through the dying all around us. Perhaps by now our wills are weaker, and our energies have flagged. But now that HIV-positive can mean living, *not* dying, surely we are needed – called to reassemble the shattered ranks of something as fragile and as vital as … community.

Survivor

My first professional job: as Knight at the Round Table

THIS BUSINESS WE CALL SHOW

"The costumes, the scenery, the make-up the props ... the audiences that lifts you when you're down ..."

– Irving Berlin, *Annie Get Your Gun*

*S*hortly after *Mame* closed, I was back to performing in dinner theater. And I'm not talking good dinner theater. I'm talking $1.98 dinner theater, the kind where on the opening night of *Camelot* they were still making our second act costumes during the first act, which meant I'd never had a chance to try mine on.

After Act One, I went into the kitchen of the theater to change into my costume, basically a breastplate-like piece of metal (armor) attached to a long piece of fabric (cape). I strode proudly on stage to be knighted as Sir Lancelot of the Round Table. But as I knelt before King Arthur, the "armor" hit my knee and went up over my head, like a turtle's head disappears into its shell. Well, I started to laugh (because I'm weak), as did the cast and some of the audience.

So there I am, shaking with laughter in my shell, trying to figure out how to save the moment. I decided to stand up, make a sweeping gesture with my cape and stride off stage. I stood, my head popped back out of the armor, I turned to toss my cape – and it wouldn't move. During my kitchen costume change, the back of my cape had somehow acquired some unexpected ballast: a big slab of roast beef.

Yes, it really happened. So much for the glamour of show business. Since then, I've played the role of Lancelot a half dozen more times, and whether it's at a Higganum, Connecticut dinner theater with a broken-down upright piano or on the stage of Carnegie Hall with a full symphony orchestra, it's always a pleasure to sing "If Ever I Would Leave You." Just hold the roast beef.

The truth about most theatrical careers is that we do different jobs for different reasons. Some are for money, some for visibility, some to work with a particular director; some to simply fill out your resume, some to qualify for insurance, and some just to stay busy and productive enough that your self-esteem doesn't sink too low, audition after audition. But once in a while, we get to do a job just for the sake of art. Miraculous.

I am not one of those actors who enjoys the rehearsal process. I want to jump on the stage and perform – Now! Applause, as nice as it may be in the moment is not the real gratification. That comes with the knowledge that for at least a few moments, you are able to transport someone, taking them to a different place and somehow, hopefully, lifting their lives and consciousness.

For most musical theatre actors, unemployment is a chronic condition. So when you get a job, you stick with it. At least I do. The truth is, I just love to sing. I always have. And, it's one of the few untroubled parts of my family heritage. In childhood, when most kids were out on their bikes, I was listening to my mother's enormous collections of original cast recordings, standing on the piano bench as if it were a stage.

By the time I was in high school, I was hopelessly hooked on the idea of being a Broadway leading man. But it wasn't until my senior year of college, during a workshop at the Los Angeles Civic Light Opera, that my life was launched toward that future with one simple conversation. I had become friends with a workshop instructor, singer-actor Marti Rolph. One day near the end of our studies, she took me to lunch and, looking me straight in the eye, gave me this counsel: "Lose weight, deal with your sexuality, finish college, move to New York and be a leading man. That's what you're meant to do with your life." It was like the "light-bulb-above-the-head" moment immortalized in cartoons. Finally, someone had said the words – out loud, at just the right time – giving me permission to do what I already knew I must. And so I determined to head to Manhattan and to become as successful as my inspirational father and my favorite Broadway musical stars – or both.

To smooth my arrival in New York, Marti had done me two more, enormous favors: She had sublet her apartment to me while she was on the road touring with *The King and I* – and, she had gotten me an appointment with a casting director at ad agency Ogilvy/Mather.

My second day in town, I called on the casting director, a nice man who seemed mildly amused with my naiveté. I told him I didn't have an agent and asked if he knew any who might be interested. He laughed; I realized just how bold I had been and apologized. But he just kept laughing, picked up the phone and called his friend Michael Hartig, a veteran agent. "Michael, I've got this kid in my office. I don't know whether he's any good or not, but I think you should see him."

I, a tall, sharp-featured blond with an almost military bearing strode into Michael Hartig's office. Michael looked up from his desk: "Oh my God, you're the one who killed my people," he said. I froze. The other agents laughed, and

I joined them, shedding my German Hitler Youth starch. Michael had me sing; after a couple of songs, he signed on to represent me. In my youthful arrogance, I thought, "Well, this isn't very hard!"

Michael called a couple of days later to send me on my first audition: to sing for Allen Jay Lerner for the part of Freddie in the Broadway revival of *My Fair Lady*. As it turned out, I was deemed too young for the part. But the feedback was good and Michael kept sending me out on great auditions. I started taking his acting class and he became a good friend as well as early mentor. Subsequently, I've learned that with most agents, you are as good as your last job. But I will always be grateful to Michael and my current agents who have stuck by me, whether I book jobs or not, or whether I am available, or not.

When I arrived in New York, I was blissfully ignorant. I did not realize that that I was a couple of decades too late for the Broadway I'd hoped to find. Despite some early success, like most performers I had to take "day jobs" to support myself. I learned quickly about the disparity and roller-coaster existence of the realties of life as a working actor. And I did everything. I waited tables, cleaned houses, was a singing bartender, was a dispatcher for a car service and a personal assistant. But probably my most humiliating job was being a singing Christmas tree … door to door, branches, lights and all. I learned to stay clear of all approaching dogs.

I had been playing "Queer Eye for the Straight Guy" long before the TV show, bullying my friends and family in their homes. Finally, someone suggested I turn it into a business, and so I did. I started a business called 'Designs on You' (borrowed from my friend, Neil Cohen) and had a great time.

There were plenty of workaday "show biz" jobs, too: singing in smoke-filled rooms to the accompaniment of the bartender's blender; acting in tacky dinner clubs and forgettable regional theaters. But at last I had the great fortune to make my Broadway debut playing opposite Angela Lansbury, my Patrick to her *Mame*. And across the footlights of the Gershwin Theater, eight times a week I got to sing to her that wonderful Jerry Herman song, "My Best Girl."

I went on to do just about every romantic lead ever written. It's actually a great job: You get to sing beautiful music, wear great costumes and play out an entire relationship. You meet the person, you go after them, you make love, you fight, you make up, you make love again, you live happily ever after – and then you get paid and go home. Perfect.

Although I've made my living playing romantic characters, I feel a bit of a fraud – kind of like the guy in the commercial who says, "I'm not a doctor, but I play one on TV." As well as I might play out romance on stage, I can't seem to make it work in real life. I'm not terribly smooth. I don't always know just the right thing to say at the right moment, or how to make the perfect gesture.

I'm hardly a poster boy for long-lasting relationships – and yet, I pulled that off on stage. The longest run I did, five glorious years, was as the romantic lead Raoul in "the little *Phantom* play."

Phantom of the Opera fans are like no others; they come back and back and back. It was a great job, perhaps the best job I've ever had – and it allowed me to roll up what in baseball parlance would be some really outstanding stats. In the course of 1,700 performances, I kissed 12,000 leading lady lips, nibbled 36,000 fingers, and sang "Christine, Christine" 72,000 times. I lifted roughly 48,000 pounds of leading lady, not including the gowns. Remember the scene when the Phantom has snatched Christine, and Raoul follows them by leaping from a bridge? The 1,700 times I did that stunt leap, all told, added up to about three times the height of the Empire State Building.

Not every stunt or star turn goes off flawlessly, however. I'd had my share of "wardrobe malfunctions" long before Janet Jackson appropriated that phrase. Many seemed to center on the wigs that helped transform me from contemporary Byron into a swain from some other era. One night in *The Phantom of the Opera*, during a particularly passionate embrace, my wig got caught on my lady love's sleeve. I stood up and the wig went down, in a fluffy heap on the floor. There may be nothing in theater less romantic than a 6'3" baritone in pin curls and a wig cap.

In another performance of that show, in the scene where I was a condemned man singing my last with a noose around my neck, a stray pyrotechnic set my wig on fire. There I was, patting out the flames, singing in the noose, still trying to hit the B flat while trying to be ... well hung.

Most of the public has no idea just how hazardous being a leading man can be. Of course, there are the obvious dangers. Kissing leading ladies is one of the greatest cripplers of leading men. No mount of swabbing or rinsing will save you if Julie Jordan has been exposed to the company cold, and she's coming right at you for the clinch after "If I Loved You." During a season in summer stock, I worked with one resident soprano we nicknamed Mono-Mona, who felled four leading men before Labor Day.

The audience also misses the under-the-breath mutterings going on during the scenes, and especially in the romantic clinches. For instance, as I take Christine's face gently in my hands to sing "All I Ask Of You," she might quietly say, "You bastard, you had a caesar salad for lunch!" And even from the front-row seats, playgoers might not notice the necessity for me to tuck the nipple of a particularly perky bosom back into milady's décolletage.

Coming up in the profession, many of us assumed there'd be a natural progression in the roles we'd play. You'd start by doing Rolf in *The Sound of Music* and Matt in *The Fantasticks*, followed by Curley in *Oklahoma* and Billy Bigelow in *Carousel*. Gracefully you'd make the transition from Lancelot to King Arthur in *Camelot*, Lieutenant Cable to Emile de Becque in *South Pacific*, followed by Don Quixote de la Mancha. Then, in the winter of your performing life you would cap off your career with Mr. Lundie in *Brigadoon* or the Starkeeper in *Carousel*. Then, finally the role you've prepared your whole career for: the role of Mr. Bedpan at the Actors Fund Home in Englewood, New Jersey.

But in my era, the lot of leading men has been a rather different one from that which I expected when I arrived in New York. I had grown up listening to guys like Gordon MacRea, Howard Keel, Harve Presnell, Alfred Drake and John Raitt. Big guys with big voices. Uncomplicated men who were what they seemed to be, with golden throats and shoulders of steel. I emulated them – I swaggered, posed, sang loud. And that was enough. I did not dance, I did not wear cat suits or sing in falsetto…

And I did, all in all, have a remarkable run of remarkable runs, exciting and fulfilling and memorable. In "this business we call show," no great role lasts forever, or even long enough. But when you are working, it's magic.

Having just finished the little *Phantom* play, I was pretty full of myself … and experiencing a professional arrogance that comes with youth and assumed professional immortality. I was armed with an invincible demeanor, but not for long.

A long time friend, Stephen Lehew, a tenor with a gorgeous voice and spirit to match, had been singing for a number of years with Marvin Hamlisch, multi-award-winning composer of film and Broadway hits. Confined to bed with the flu and no voice, Stephen called to ask if I'd sub for him at a concert with Mr. Hamlisch – in three days.

"Cool," I thought. Marvin Hamlisch. Pretty heady stuff. The man was a legend and whether it was one job or a valuable contact for the future, it sounded good to me. So I jumped in a cab and arrived at his palatial apartment overlooking Central Park, where Academy Awards gleamed from the shelves and photos of him with the celebrities and dignitaries of our time covered the walls. I sang for him.

We chatted a bit about pets … his wife was charming … and I remember leaving feeling good about our first encounter. He seemed pleased with my voice, handed me a copy of his song and said "Learn this, and I'll see you in Washington, D.C. on Sunday."

At the time I was doing an Off-Broadway cabaret with my pal Bonnie Franklin and we had a dreadful schedule of weekend shows. After a very late Saturday night performance I got on the shuttle for Washington D.C. early Sunday morning. I'd coached the song with a musical director friend of mine and thought I'd learned it – *thought* being the operative word.

When I arrived at the Ritz Carlton in the early afternoon, I met with the stage manager and went to the performance space. The ballroom had been set up with a thousand chairs all pointing toward a round clearing in the center. There, on a round revolving stage covered in flowers, was a beautiful Steinway grand piano. It looked like a gigantic musical wedding cake.

Mr. Hamlisch, for reasons still unknown, declined to come down for a sound check, so I never had a chance to rehearse the song with him. Because different pianists have very different styles it was, at best, risky – but I had no choice. So I took a nap and waited for the festivities to begin.

After a black tie dinner for a bazillion dollars a plate, Mr. Hamlisch came out and did a 45-minute "and then I wrote" kind of show – all very impressive, polished and entertaining, concluding with selections from perhaps his greatest claim to fame, *A Chorus Line*. He then spoke about a recent trip to India where, after having met the Dalai Lama, he'd been inspired to write the next piece, titled "One Song." After some self-deprecating remark about his own singing abilities, he told the audience he'd brought along a friend from New York to sing "One Song" and introduced me.

I walked down the endless aisle with my most confident stride, and took the microphone. As the lights shifted focus from the piano to me, the stage began to revolve – and Mr. Hamlisch proceeded to play an introduction that sounded nothing like the song I had in my head. I went totally blank.

If you ever saw Albert Brooks in the film *Broadcast News*, you know what I mean by the theatrical term "flop sweat." It's as if someone is pouring a bucket of water from the top of your head while you simultaneously gush sweat from pores you never wanted to know you had. It is also accompanied by a sinking feeling in your stomach that leaves you certain you will go through the floor at any minute … except that your head is so light and the nausea so overwhelming that the rush of senses leaves you immobile.

I couldn't remember a single word. Not one. Out of desperation I began to make up stellar lyrics like "Night draws nigh … you and I … piece of pie … on my thigh" – anything that came into my head to fill the endless void in which I was drowning. It is a beautiful song that I now know backwards and forwards. In fact, the minute I left the stage I could have sung it beautifully … but not with the totally unfamiliar accompaniment I was hearing.

About half way through, I decided to "lay out" for a few bars, thinking perhaps I could get back on track and finish the song triumphantly. But all the optimism, prayer and creativity I could muster couldn't save that moment. When I stopped singing, I looked over at Mr. Hamlisch, who was now making a valiant effort to "fill" the enormous spaces I was leaving. It went down hill from there.

It was an arrangement that had many modulations … where the keys seemed to get higher and higher and higher building to a crescendo and high note that on any other occasion would not have been a problem for me to hit. But by this time I was so upset and my throat had tightened to the point that not only did I not hit the note … I totally yodeled. I don't mean a little crack in the voice that a good friend might say "Oh don't worry, I'm sure no one noticed but me." I'm talking about a resounding, frightening vocal spasm, a yodel so disturbing that I could see people in the audience shudder and grimace. But their discomfort was nothing compared to the mortification I was feeling.

After what seemed an eternity, Mr. Hamlisch stood from the piano. As we took our bow, he said so quietly that only I could hear, "You are so out of here!" I left the stage, went back to my room and promptly got sick. But the worst was yet to come. Although I'd flown down, I was supposed to ride back in a car with Mr. Hamlisch and his personal assistant.

Now, if I'd been a smart person, I would have spent the night at the hotel and flown home the next day. But in the flurry of emotion and because everyone was in such a hurry to leave, I threw my things in the back of the limousine and climbed in. With a look of total innocence and mystification, Mr. Hamlisch asked "So, what happened?" It appeared he had no sense that he bore any responsibility for the fiasco. So I simply replied, "Well, I guess I was under-rehearsed" and let it go at that.

It was an excruciating ride from DC to New York. I spent most of the time feigning sleep till we pulled up to my apartment building. I said good night to the driver and before I slunk to my apartment, I took aside the very nice assistant (who had been most understanding and apologetic) and poured out my heart. "I have been on stage my entire life, I've sung with dozens of symphony orchestras, I've done more than 1,500 performances of *The Phantom of the Opera* and countless other shows and reviews – and never, *never* in my life has anything like this happened to me!" I handed her the check I'd been given, saying I could not in good conscience cash it, and asking that she donate it to the organization for which we performed.

Needless to say, I've never been asked to sing with Mr. Hamish again. And for days I would wake up in a cold sweat and sick to my stomach. But I learned a valuable lesson: You never can be too prepared or over-rehearsed. In Alec Guinness' brilliant theatrical memoir *Blessings in Disguise*, there is a chapter titled "The Readiness Is All." After 25 years in the business, if I hadn't known it before, that night I learned that we are all dependent on each other. And unless you live in a vacuum, readiness depends both on personal preparation and the support of those with whom you work. No one does it alone.

So I've chalked it off as a learning experience. But I've also, somehow, never managed since then to listen to the soundtrack for *A Chorus Line*.

Early Beginnings...

Howard McGillen, current Phantom on Broadway,
me and Leslie Uggums on a Theater Guild Cruise.

There truly are no people like show people!
Linda Ellerbee, Whoopi, and me being silly after a
Halloween night playing poker at Whoopi's home.

Tom Jones

Summer Stock with John Raitt…

One Last Dance ... Granny & Me

FAMILY ALBUM

"Love and marriage, love and marriage ... go together like a horse and carriage. This I tell you brother, you can't have one without the ... other"

– "Love and Marriage," Sammy Cahn and Jimmy Van Heusen.

*W*ell, very little in my family history has anything to do with these lyrics. Nothing about either of Mother's parents was conventional or dependable. My grandmother, Eva, was one of twelve children; her mother, Alice, was an heiress of the Mayhew family who monopolized the 'fishing smacks' in Yarmouth, England. It was a home of strictly- controlled privilege. At an early age, Alice had been presented at court and, with her skills at embroidery and costume design, found favor with the aging dowager Queen Victoria.

But Alice's season in that society ended abruptly when she married Charles Barnett. He was a handsome rascal, a soloist with the Welsh Men's Choir, but was categorically rejected by the Mayhew family for social, economic and most importantly, religious reasons. Disinherited by her family and excommunicated from her church, Alice and Charles decided to leave England for Montreal. Immediately following the christening of daughter Eva at Westminster Abby, they sailed for new beginnings in Canada. It was an auspicious beginning for a woman who would prove to be the source of notoriety and intrigue.

Eva spent her early years at the foot of Mt. Royal in Montreal, until employment with the Canadian Pacific Railroad dictated a move for the Barnett clan to Vancouver. There as a teenager, Eva met a friend of her eldest brother. Andrew McKay Martin was energetic and displayed an ebullient and persuasive style. He courted Eva in an enthusiastic whirlwind and they eloped to Alaska where they lived, as my grandmother later described it, "from one ice flow to another." During that year, their first daughter, Alice, was born. In 1919, while on an extended vacation to Southern California, Andrew decided it was the land of opportunity. And so they stayed. My Grandfather first worked for the phone company and later in the oil fields, while Granny cared for Alice who was already showing signs of an illness that would keep her mind at the level of a four-year-old for the 57 years of her life.

The young Martins saw that, indeed, this was a land of wide-open possibilities. It was the era of young Hollywood and Chinatown. Nothing was out of reach with their ambition, charm and beauty. Eva began working as the credit manager with the Brunswick Music Company and, being an accomplished pianist who sang, demonstrated the newest songs available in sheet music.

Andrew supplemented their income in the burgeoning oil fields with the Southern California Edison Company. Later, he sold his stock to begin his own business, the Wilco Company; one of five plastics corporations he created in his lifetime, it would bring him uncommon wealth and all the challenges and temptations that go with it.

They were both energetic, ambitious, charming and creative – but also jealous and possessive, busy in their own careers while raising two daughters. It was apparent early on that Andrew was not capable of being faithful, despite his adoration of his vivacious young bride. Their ambitions and egos collided in an irreversible explosion; their daughter Ann (my mother) saw her world turn upside down by their messy divorce. And it was all front page news, because of the notoriety of the players.

Eva, proud and bold, declared her independence. Deeply wounded and distant from the comfort of her family, she became what was far from common in that era, a single mother. Despite their divorce, Andrew remained the love of her life. Throughout her life, she kept a picture of him next to her bed. Not long before her death she confided to me, "If I had it to do over, I would have handled things differently. I was not wise in the ways of the world and too proud."

But personal reversals did not stop her. Nor did the Great Depression. She supplemented her work at the music company by working at a switchboard, giving dancing lessons and for a time she ran what she admitted was one of the worst diners in Hollywood. Her infectious sense of humor and charismatic grace propelled her upward in the world of finance, where she ultimately became the Financial Controller for the Los Angeles Department of Water and Power. Pretty heady stuff for a woman of that time. She was surrounded by men like Bill Mulholland and William Randolph Hearst. She not only held her own, but shone like a star. Around town and in the press, she was known as "Queen Eva" and graced the social columns regularly.

Whether as a regular guest at Hearst Castle or dancing on her lunch hour at the Coconut Grove at the Ambassador Hotel, Eva had the pluck and ability to balance work, home and a fairly active and public social life. In the meantime, Andrew had become an entrepreneurial maverick with an immense ego and fortune to match. He was wildly ambitious, creative and ultimately charming. After six years of attempts at reconciliation with Eva, he finally married a woman he called his "Yankee Pride," Ruth (who we grandchildren later called Mummy-Pat) and they had a son. Andrew had a "Henry Higgins complex" and tried to remake both Ruth and eventually his third wife, Mary, into the image that suited him and the social circles his business required. His controlling nature extended beyond his wives to children, grandchildren and other family members.

After her divorce from Andrew, Eva remained single for 11 years and broke more than a few hearts along the way. Mother used to tell me stories of covering for Granny who was engaged, at one point, to three different men. She was wined and dined, courted and celebrated in the glittering society of the political and theatrical stars of the day. She determined to never again be dominated or tied to just one man – until she met David Lytell Hutton. Dashing, dapper and exuding enormous confidence, he was already both famous and infamous; famous, because he had been a vaudeville headliner (at the Palace Theater in New York City) and sung in New York's Grand Opera. His name appeared in the first edition of the show business publication Variety – Volume One, Issue # 1. He had an imposing bass-baritone voice; Will Rogers reportedly once called him "a big man around town in a local kind of way."

He was infamous, because at an earlier age he had been married to the controversial evangelist Aimee Semple McPherson – his first marriage, her third. Several years David's senior, Aimee brought him to her Angelus Temple to produce religious operas. But she also saw different possibilities. Having just emerged from a notoriously acclaimed "kidnapping" incident and sensationalized courtroom battle, her reputation had been damaged. And while still worshiped by her flock, she, despite her very public life, was painfully alone. When I interviewed Aimee's daughter, Roberta, she said that Aimee always said she "kissed her shoulder goodnight."

Controversy erupted again when Aimee and my Grandfather eloped to Yuma and were married in a plane. All very theatrical and well planned for the benefit of the press. There had long been questions about Aimee's authenticity versus her (and now their) extravagant and "unseemly" lifestyle. Though long before their marriage Aimee had been the source of curiosity and derision, she was without doubt the most famous woman of her time. And the services at Angelus Temple were the best show in town. Together, Aimee and David's theatrical antics on and off the church platform were cause for widespread gossip and envy. It was their custom, after a weekend of exhausting church activities for a live congregation of thousands as well as countless more watching on television, to travel in their Dusenberg from their palatial home by Angelus Temple to their

Moroccan-style castle at Lake Elsinore. The contrast between their lavish lifestyle and the modest means of their congregants was not a flattering one.

Anthony Quinn was quoted as saying that "Aimee single-handedly fed the Mexican-American community during the Depression." There are countless stories of her affairs with celebrities, he among them. Though her lifestyle may have been an issue for some, her faith was real, her abilities to heal, heralded. Again, when I had the pleasure of speaking with her daughter, I asked about the 'miracles'. She replied "The whole thing about the miracles was *if you believe!*"

And as a marketing genius, Aimee was unparalleled. Like many public figures, celebrity took its toll: Seeking solace, she turned to Seconal and gin. Ultimately, David could no longer take the intrigue of church politics and being "Mr. Aimee Semple McPherson," and divorced her.

Shortly thereafter, Eva and David met at a barbecue at the home of Dr. and Mrs. Cummings. Ironically, Dr. Cummings would be the judge in a much-publicized custody battle several years later over my Mother. Their entire crowd was larger-than-life people who kept company with the likes of Mae West, Charlie Chaplin, Cecil B. DeMille, W.C. Fields, Douglas Fairbanks, and Marion Davies.

After a whirlwind courtship they eloped, again creating a press frenzy. David was good to Eva's daughters Ann and Alice. David and Eva were great pals and both enjoyed playing elaborate practical jokes on whoever crossed their path. So these two mischief-loving playmates had great fun eluding the press in order to take their vows in private.

They went to the home of David's devout parents, absconded with their tithing money, and left an IOU in its place that said simply "Sudden Notion. Love triumphant, Love, Eva and David."

LOVE TRIUMPHANT. I like that.

PARENTING A PARENT

"You are my sunshine, my only sunshine. You make me happy when skies are grey. You'll never know Dear, how much I love you. Please don't take my sunshine away."

– "You are My Sunshine," Jimmie Davis and Charles Mitchell

t was time for her first bath in my home. She stood defiantly in her floor length dressing gown – not just a robe, but a gown worthy of Loretta Young making an entrance.

"Darling, I can do this myself. I have been bathing for 87 years." Her pride was overruling the practicality of the moment. And who could blame her? A private and proud woman raised by a mother who had herself been a Lady In Waiting to Queen Victoria, my grandmother Eva retained the regal carriage of her upbringing. To my contemporary New York City apartment she brought an old world courtliness and style.

"Granny, I know this makes you nervous, but …" "I am not nervous," she shot back, her bravado cracking just a little: "I'm … embarrassed." Small wonder. In my grandmother's own home we never left our bedrooms without robe and slippers. I don't remember seeing anyone in my family naked until I was a teenager, and only then by accident.

"Well, here's the deal," I pressed on. "You need a bath and I won't let you do it alone." "Who taught you to be so particular?" she asked with just a hint of a smile breaking through. We both knew the answer and laughed. She shed her gown with a defiant air and a dramatic pose: Once my grandmother made a decision, it was final. I helped her into the tub, her body now small and frail, her humor intact, her spirit indomitable. When it came time to wash 'down there', I hesitated. Finally she looked at me with a wicked grin and said "Oh darling, don't worry, nothing down there but cobwebs!" And so with a laugh that could melt the heart of the Devil himself, she completed her toilette.

Laughter was her trademark. Her generous heart touched all whom she encountered. Her grandchildren and great-grandchildren all knew her spontaneous, affectionate gestures. And the tenants of the many rental properties she owned knew her to be a lifter of lives, nurturing, understanding and supportive.

And so, in her mid-80s, this woman who had survived three strokes following the death of my grandfather had now come to live in my home. No longer able to care for herself, she chose to sell her home (much to the amazement and dismay of our family) and move to New York to spend her final days. Neither she, our family, my friends nor I could imagine what an adventure it would be over the next two and one-half years.

The simple act of giving her now petite body a bath in my oversized tub set the stage for many of our most heartfelt and significant conversations. Because she was so small in the slippery tub, I had to hold her up, lest she slip under the bubbles. It was cause for much laughter and a forced intimacy that drew us together, allowed her to be cared for in a new way ... and taught me lessons in dependability on deeper levels than I'd ever known.

And the laughter continued. I had transformed the bedroom of my apartment into a Victorian doll house, bringing her most precious things to reproduce the bedroom from her home, from the canopy bed draped in satin and silk to the multi-layered floral drapes cut down to fit. The Tiffany chandelier ... the shelves filled with perfume bottles and framed photos of days and loved ones now gone ... the precious porcelain and crystal figures she'd collected: It all worked together to suggest a life of beauty, accomplishment and comfort. The chaise lounge was filled with the antique dolls of her childhood and the formal mahogany furniture was polished until it gleamed. In her lace-covered, quilted bed jackets, she looked like a cross between Auntie Mame and Mrs. Santa. She had arrived with 264 pairs of shoes ... cases filled with gloves (at every length, weight and style), scarves, handkerchiefs, hair ornaments, furs, hats, and enough clothes to overwhelm the best dressed women on Fifth Avenue.

You can imagine my surprise when she asked me to find her a pair of leather pants. When I asked her why, she said "Well dear, I've been looking at the fashion magazines and see women wearing them with their furs. I still look like a million in my mink and the leather would help keep me warm. Now, I don't want a tight pair like the cheap girls wear ... just a nice pair of simple pleated leather or better yet, suede slacks." So I brought home three pair for her to try ... brown, blue and bright red. She kept them all.

Next on her agenda was to cut her hair. Since her strokes it was nearly impossible for her to manage. Now you must understand that no one had *ever* seen Granny without her waist long hair piled high on her head – but she was determined. Since my attempts to style her hair for her were disastrous, she got out the scissors and said, "Either you do it or I will!" I'll never forget the sound of those sheers cutting through her thick locks. I was horrified. She was delighted. I immediately called a friend to come and style it – and I must admit she looked wonderful, the most chic grandmother in Manhattan.

The adventures we shared are a book in itself. She had almost three years of a "last hurrah" as the honorary Granny to Manhattan's Upper West Side. My friends spoiled her with visits that always included flowers, homemade soups and muffins, the scented candles and potpourri she loved, but most of all long talks and much laughter. She would listen to their tales and dole out advice with wit and wisdom. I remember one afternoon after her customary tea (with a "just a touch" of sherry) she asked my friend Jan to let down her pulled-back hair: "There, dear, that's better, with just a bit of softness around your face …" And almost without fail, she was right. Granny had a way of cutting to the chase in such a disarming manner you never thought of her insights or opinions as criticism, just loving suggestions.

We had never spoken about my sexual orientation. I knew it had to be addressed if we were going to live together. The conversation went something like this:

"Now that you're here, there is something we should discuss. I'm a healthy man and hopefully will not spend every night of my life alone. So what will happen if I ask someone to spend the night with me?"

"Darling, what you do in your bedroom is your business."

"So, if you run into someone in the hall at four in the morning, what would you do?"

"I'd say hello to him."

"What do you mean, him?"

"Darling, I've met your friends, I'm not stupid!"

"How long have you known?"

"Since you were a little boy … I just didn't know if you were ready to handle it. I've often wondered why you've never talked to me about it."

"My entire life, you have been the constant. You were always the one I could depend on, that I knew would love me no matter what. I guess I wasn't willing to risk losing you."

Patting my hand, she assured me, "Buddy, you could never lose me. I'd love you no matter what. And you're not doing anything wrong. It's more important how you love, rather than who you love. And besides, who else could dress me and decorate our home better than a gay man? You have inherited my good taste."

We let it go at that.

She did enjoy the finer things in life and attacked Manhattan with relish. From tea at the Helmsley Palace, to visits to Tiffany's and Bergdorf's, to our last dinner at Tavern on the Green (by way of a horse drawn carriage) where she consumed three dozen oysters and champagne, she charmed even the most jaded New Yorkers with the twinkle in her eye and her still flirtatious smile. We'd go for walks (she in the tapestry-upholstered wheel chair I'd had made for her) in Central Park, where she insisted on riding the carousel. Then we'd head past the zoo for Frozen Hot Chocolate at Serendipity's. Did I also mention she loved the hot dogs on the street with extra mustard and sauerkraut? She delighted in everything and everyone. Not that she suffered fools gladly – but she had come to a point in life where she cheerfully exhibited more tolerance than I could muster on my best day.

She delighted in seeing "The Nutcracker" at Lincoln Center and the New York Philharmonic at Carnegie Hall. But the sweetest times were those just curled up in her canopy bed playing Monopoly (she always won), or dining together as she graciously abided my dreadful attempts at cooking. She no longer liked wearing her false teeth when we were alone, and doctors' orders said she could have no sugar, salt or fatty foods – so mostly, we cheated!

Lest I give the impression it was all fun and games, it was not, for either of us. There were challenges. Medicare, medication, multiple doctor visits with various specialists, stroke rehabilitation, family uncertainties, financial decisions, keeping her occupied and entertained. We had to make peace with her increasing fears and dependency, and the inevitable conversations about mortality, regrets and the "what ifs" that plague those whose worlds are getting smaller and more frightening. But mostly, we'd come out of these uncertainties with laughter. I remember when it came time for her to acknowledge her need for adult diapers, she took it with good humor, joking about the celebrity then hawking that product on TV: "Well, if it's good enough for June Allyson …" That night while she slept I painted her toenails bright red, which she'd always thought vulgar. She never said a word, but somehow my coffee tasted strangely of vinegar the next morning. And so it went.

Most work out of town, I turned down. But I did accept a summer stock tour in *Annie Get Your Gun,* playing Annie Oakley's husband Frank Butler opposite Bonnie Franklin (star of the CBS TV series "One Day at a Time").

We were to play two venues in the Poconos and in Buck's County, both in Pennsylvania. So I packed my car complete with wheelchair, walker, canes, medication, Ensure and Depends, Granny's dreadful cat Gretchen – and off we went.

I rented a little cabin in the woods where we could wake up and have coffee looking at the beautiful trees by a small lake. Granny got it into her head that she wanted to go for a swim in the lake. Mind you, she hadn't been in the pool of her own home for 20 years. But off I went in search of a bathing suit. When we went to put it on … how to say this in a genteel manner … oh hell, I can't. Her breasts were so long we couldn't get them to stay in the cups. We laughed till we cried and she wet herself. Finally, with a resigned giggle, she said, "Oh dear, just throw them over my shoulders and we'll call them water wings" – and we went skinny dipping instead. What a sight that must have been.

The first time Granny met Bonnie, we went to dinner with her husband Marvin Minoff, a movie producer from Hollywood. I'd never met him and barely knew Bonnie. After a martini or two, Granny regaled us with the most embarrassing stories of my childhood. At one point a family entered with a child on what I call a leash, one of those shoulder harnesses attached to a long chord. Bonnie commented on how terrible she thought it was. Granny replied "Oh, I always had to keep Buddy (she always called me that) on a leash, or he'd run off. But I always knew where to find him, especially at I Magnin's in Beverly Hills. He'd always be in the millenary department trying on all the ladies' hats." I went under the table. Marvin covered his face with his hands; Bonnie looked at me with a sympathetic smile, but I feared she was thinking, "THIS is the person who's supposed to sweep me off my feet and be my new leading man?" All this unnoticed by Granny. She just went on telling all the stories I never wanted anyone to hear.

Life with Granny yielded so many tales, from outrageous to inspiring: Her consumption, by mistake, of marijuana brownies … the visit to the Statue of Liberty where she stood up from her wheelchair with her hand over her heart and recited the Pledge of Allegiance … serving as the laughing prop when friends and I played 'spin the Granny' with her in her wheelchair …

But the best tale of all is about Easter Sunday. When I was growing up, every year I would get a new white suit for Easter, usually with short pants. This was not a good look on a fat kid, but it was tradition. On Granny's first Easter in New York, I'd invited a few friends over for coffee before we went to services at Riverside Church, and then on to The Oak Room at the Plaza for brunch. After getting Granny bathed and dressed, I was rushing around getting everything ready. I jumped in the shower and as I was tying my tie she came in and said "Darling, I don't like that tie."

That was a shocker because she always was very complimentary of everything I wore and how I looked. She continued: "As a matter of fact, I don't care for what you're wearing at all."

Running out of patience and time, I snapped, "Okay, fine, what do you want me to wear?" She padded, gold tipped cane and all, back to her bedroom and proudly returned with a suit bag. She had, with the help of one of my friends, ordered me a white linen suit – and had the pants cut off. She'd even bought me a new white shirt and lavender tie. She was so proud and happy. I was horrified. But I feigned delight and put it on. The most difficult dilemma was trying to decide what the hell shoes to wear with an outfit like that.

My friends arrived moments later and as I opened the door I warned, "Not a word – not a single word!" To their credit, they managed to stifle their remarks in front of Granny. But you can only imagine the looks we got: There I was, a 33- year-old, 6'3" man dressed as a cross between Lord Fauntleroy and an Easter bunny, walking his grandmother down the center aisle of Riverside Church with 10-12 friends trailing behind, crying with laughter. But Granny was so proud – of me, of her accomplishment, and of being the center of attention – that it was worth it all. After church, we headed downtown to the Plaza, where our long table of actors sang a rousing chorus of "Easter Parade" in what was otherwise a rather sedate, quiet room. Thanks to the combination of my attire and our merriment, the manager remembered me for years thereafter.

Nothing could throw Granny. She handled every challenge that came her way during those years with humor and grace. As she always quoted to me, "To whom much is given, much is expected." She also regularly admonished me with a peculiar British expression: "Keep your pecker up, darling!" It was her way of telling me to keep my chin up – and to this day, I recall that guidance with a smile, and try to follow it.

Morning Coffee
With Granny & me in my kitchen

MY ROMANCE

"Say you'll share with me one love, one lifetime. Anywhere
you go let me go too.
That's all I ask of you ... All I want is freedom, a world
with no more night ... and
you, always beside me, to guard me and to guide me ...
share each day with me
each night, each morning. That's all I ask of you."

– "All I Ask of You," *The Phantom of the Opera*, Andrew Lloyd Webber

I sang those lyrics in more than 1,700 performances of *Phantom*, and even more in concerts around the world. They articulated what I wanted in my own life, but a long-lasting relationship has eluded me. Maybe it's my vision of that relationship – idealized, I'll admit – that accounts for my single status.

Across the years, I have loved often, but never lightly. I have loved well, and been well-loved ... though not unconditionally. To use the theatrical term, I've never managed long runs in relationships. My romantic history – a series of relatively-brief, monogamous relationships with long stretches of solo life in-between – is best described in this snippet of verse from Dorothy Parker: "Life is an endless cycle of song, a medley of extemporania. And love is a thing that can never go wrong – and I am Marie of Rumania."

Whenever I'm asked, "What is your favorite song?" the answer has always been: "Any love song ever written." Most people who know me will tell you that I'm a hopeless romantic, so it came as no surprise to my dearest friends when I released a CD of love songs, "Byron Nease: Listen To My Heart." A particularly candid friend suggested a cover photo for the CD that would realistically express my experience of being in love, "but you couldn't get both the camera in and your head in the oven."

Off stage, I'm not terribly smooth. I don't always know just the right thing to say at the right moment, exactly when or how to make the "perfect gesture." And once involved, I tend to become this person that I don't begin to recognize or particularly admire. I guess that's why I relate to the characters that don't always get it quite right – guys like Harold Hill, Professor Higgens, and Max Sennett in *Mack and Mabel.*

But because I can pull it off on a big stage, I'll still go on singing my love songs – because the truth is, I'm not a hopeless romantic, I'm a hopeful one. Despite the disappointments, there have been wonderful moments in my romantic life when I've felt the most fully human and alive, connected and spiritually ful-filled in the arms of someone I loved and who loved me. One of my sweetest memories is the first significant relationship I had in New York, when I was in my mid-20s.

During a coaching session with musical director David Lewis, I was thumb-ing through a photo album and saw a snapshot of Bill. After I groveled a bit, David made a call and set us up on a blind date. Bill was a few years older than I, sophisticated, worldly, smart, funny and handsome. We both remember that when he opened the door to his apartment, I audibly gasped. It was an instant and powerful connection for me. Beyond the physical, I had a sense that I knew this man, a recognition of spirit that was intoxicating.

I was in bliss. Bill was less certain. My apartment became a place where I picked up mail and changed clothes, as we spent the better part of two years together. When I wasn't pursuing my career or commuting to Los Angeles to take care of Granny and Gramp, most of my time was spent with him. He had a beautiful little penthouse on Riverside Drive that overlooked the Hudson River. I entered his world of photography and sophisticated friends, fascinated by this New York circle I'd never known. His community was interesting and diverse, and his world specific to his tastes and interests. But mostly, I was just overwhelm-ingly in love with him.

After we'd been seeing each other a few months, I gave him a surprise birth-day party. I raided his phone book, invited all his friends and went all out. It was a great success. He was truly surprised and delighted. At the end of the evening, I was exhausted. I remember crawling into bed and he patted his chest and said "Now, you come here and be my guest." I'll never forget that feeling of being "home" with a partner, perhaps for the first time in my life. In the long run, we didn't work out. But I'm grateful today to count Bill and his partner as close friends.

There have been other people I felt, and hoped, would be "the one." But so far, it has not played out that way and though there are no real holes in my life, I always seem to be on the lookout. I have this old-fashioned notion about love: I believe in commitment and monogamy.

With one exception, in all my relationships, no one has ever been faithful. I find this to be amazing, especially because I have been so clear, specific and up-front about my boundaries. The option of open relationships has always seemed to me to be fraught with risk.

Friends would say that I have pretty consistently chosen difficult partners. I often feel that where my heart goes is beyond my powers of reason or choice – but I'm willing to give some thought to the reasons I may have chosen badly. I'm also willing to consider the slight possibility – okay, the virtual certainty – that I'm not exactly "low maintenance" myself. Even with that, I think I have a lot to offer, and so I persevere. Anne Rice: *"If love were a choice, who would choose such exquisite pain?"* I would.

And yet I see myself as Noel Coward did in his poem, "I Am No Good at Love":

"I am no good at love, my heart should be wise and free.

But I kill the unfortunate golden goose, whoever it may be,

with over-articulate tenderness and too much intensity.

I am no good at love, I betray it with little sins.

For I fear the bitterness of the end in the moment that it begins.

And the bitterness of the last goodbye, is the bitterness that wins."

In my much-married family, infidelity has plagued and defined four generations. So it has always been a "hot spot" for me, and still is.

A few years ago I spent the evening of July 4th with my friend Fran Weaver in her high-rise building that had a terrace with a 180 degree view of Pueblo, Colorado. Fran was excited to share the spectacular display of fireworks going on all over her city. We watched so many celebrations dotting the landscape, at stadiums, schools, backyards and parks – folks spread out across her county, celebrating a sense of belonging to one community, one family, one nation.

After about five minutes I felt so anxious I could hardly breathe, excused myself and escaped to the quiet of her living room. I knew instantly what was upsetting me, and after putting my feelings in order, I returned to the terrace and told my confidante Fran this story.

In 1994 I met Phillip: tall, handsome, engaging, seductive. Phillip was in the midst of editing a book about gay and lesbian role models, essays in words and photographs. It was a wonderful book and I was impressed by him and his seeming desire to make a contribution – to celebrate the uncommon, everyday heroes and positive values in the gay community, which is so often perceived to be focused on self-indulgence and other unhealthy behavior.

I had just created my one-man show *From the Parsonage to Broadway* and was going into churches to sing and speak about what it's like to grow up gay in the church. I thought that Phillip and I would make a good team, that we shared a desire to make a difference in the world.

We – or, in retrospect, I – fell fast and hard. Through a series of rather complicated logistical circumstances, we wound up living together very quickly, rings and all. Truthfully, early on I had all the clues I needed to know something was amiss. But I was swept away in the tidal wave of romance and ignored the information at hand. Denial? Perhaps. Willful? Definitely. Hopeful? Absolutely!

On July 4th in the year we met, I spent the day moving Phillip from his sublet into my apartment in Manhattan. I felt uneasy that day about a 'friend' Phillip had helping him move; their communication was flirtatious and to me, disconcerting. But I pushed through the day, certain that once we were ensconced in our home, all else would fall away and we'd be happy and content. As I said, I'm an old-fashioned guy, and had been very clear about boundaries I need in a relationship. Late that afternoon, Phillip put me on a plane to sing a concert date. I hoped we were okay. We were not.

The next day I received an awkward, well-intentioned call from a friend who had seen Phillip and his "friend" in a compromising situation in a public place the evening I left. When I confronted him, he admitted that they'd spent the evening together watching the fireworks, that they were attracted to one another – but he claimed there was only a kiss, and he'd told this fellow that it could go no further because he was committed to me. I wanted to believe him, so I did.

I went full speed ahead and did my best to build a home for the two of us, paying all the bills – even many for his home-based business – but not paying the slightest bit of attention to the clues. I realize now, we wanted different things: I wanted a partner, he wanted a staff.

In fairness, I'd like to think he did love me to the degree he was capable. But ultimately, he betrayed me in every way possible. I had let myself be borne along by the "fireworks" of our union, and ignored the apprehensions and instincts I felt in the depths of my soul.

So many men have what I call a "Clintonian" sense of entitlement when it comes to sexual infidelity. I can't help but wonder if Phillip thought he could convince me to soften my convictions about the importance of monogamy – or if he just thought I'd look the other way. Ultimately, I could do neither. As our financial situation as well as our personal relationship deteriorated, I had to get out. Integrity and dependability are everything to me. And, I'd never been so lonely, as when we were living together.

A couple of years ago we were able to spend some time together and mend some of our fences. But two things became clear: what it was that made me fall in love with him, and why it could never work. I still found him to be completely lovable. But this time, I could see him as undependable in terms of my expectations for a partner – and I could see how he, in turn, found me rigid in those expectations. For the first time, I understood my role in setting up the dynamics of our relationship. I have held onto that realization, and tried to learn from it. But I've also held onto precious moments from our time together, like an evening at the movies when the simple act of his hand caressing my neck made me feel so completely connected.

Again from Anne Rice, her book *Violin*: *"I was dazed with old love. Or love that is everlasting."* Once I love someone, there remains a place in my heart that is always in love with them that never changes, no matter the outcome.

But there's also much more room in my heart, and I'm eager and ready to fill it. I want once again to feel the exhilaration of that first embrace. I'd like the confidence and dependability of knowing that someone is watching my back; someone to spoil me a little in the small ways in which I've enjoyed spoiling those I've loved. I want to be cherished, to wake up and have coffee and *The New York Times* in bed with someone I admire, who makes me laugh and makes me want to be a better man … for him and for me. And as generous as I can be in some areas of my world, there are parts of a relationship where I absolutely do not want to share him with anyone else.

And, so, though I may have chosen badly in the past, I hope that one day if Prince Charming storms up on his white steed, my experience will allow me to recognize him. I realize at this point in my life, that beyond the challenges of taking care of family, an insane schedule of travel and irregular work hours, not to mention the baggage that I have brought into my relationships, I have set up standards that are virtually impossible for anyone to live up to. I have been a participant in co-creating my relationships, good and bad.

There is a lyric from RENT that rings true: "I'm just looking for someone whose baggage matches mine."

I believe in "Happily Ever After." I have to.

TOTEM POLE TOWEL RACKS

*"Money, you should forgive the expression, is like manure.
It doesn't do anybody any good till it's spread around helping
little things to grow."*

– Hello Dolly, Jerry Herman

*W*hen Mother saw something she wanted, it just went without saying that it belonged in our home. Whether or not we could afford anything new, it made no difference. Her collector's eye rarely regarded practicality or necessity. I know she wanted to create the most perfect and beautiful environment possible. I think she also sought to fill out an otherwise unfulfilled existence – to put things in the place of relationships.

Like Mother, I love my things. But to me, they feel like pieces of my heart. I surround myself with the things that not only bring comfort, but also enrich my imagination. It is an aesthetic, but more – almost another kind of spirituality. And in the years since my HIV-positive diagnosis, it has been a way of reaffirming that life is continuing, changing, growing and moving forward. Everything I own has a story, a bit of family history or travel lore, a sentimental attachment beyond the obvious beauty or practical purpose.

Like Mother, I have the ability and desire – or curse – to make a home wherever I am. Sometimes that means re-arranging the furniture in a hotel (yes, really) or decking theatre dressing rooms with a few of my own personal effects (I don't travel light). I'm a nester, and, much to the dismay of my accountant, a collector. Recently a friend suggested I hand out printed Docent's Guides as people enter my apartment, to help them better view the volume of artifacts and photos.

Walk into my home, and you'll begin instantly to know who I am. It is an intimate expression of me. And though my styles have changed and matured as have I, my obsessive need for beauty and order has never flagged. In fact, sometimes my decorating choices have signaled who I am becoming before I was consciously aware of any change.

I've heard it said that *"Some people come into your life for a season, some for a reason, and some for a lifetime."* So do people's photos, which in my home form a changing exhibition. Some are family, some friends. Some are ancestors that keep me grounded in the rich history of my heritage. Some I frame just to make me smile. And some are of loved ones I do not want to forget. It's a way of keeping them alive in my world. There is almost a psychic presence that I experience. A reverence.

Both my apartment and my summer cottage look like crash courses in colliding cultures. There are feather headdresses from the Amazon and masks from all over Africa, one of which was used in the circumcision rites in the Congo (don't ask). There's a carved figure bought from a Ghanaian witch doctor whom I saw perform a voodoo ceremony. (He wanted an extra $50, cash, for his blessing and I've often wonder if he cursed me for eternity for declining to pay.) Eight-foot totem poles from Bali have become extravagant towel racks; six-foot totem poles from Alaska flank the stairs, and a 17-foot-long Japanese warrior banner hangs in a screened porch. I don't bring home small trinkets.

I have aboriginal art from Australia in my kitchen, Venetian glass in my dining room, Tibetan prayer scriptures framed above my bed and, across from that, an enormous photo of a Buddha in Burma. In my living room, a 17th-century Emperor's kimono hangs above a Spanish throne. There are Russian Icons, lacquer boxes and paintings, an Egyptian sarcophagus, lanterns from Japan, carpets from Turkey, coconut purses (my brilliant solution for storing plastic bags in my kitchen), a grass skirt from Tahiti (you never know), a bungee-jumping sheep, belly dancing costumes, carved canoes from New Guinea, an enormous drum from Tonga...

That partial inventory doesn't include the really useful things like the delicacies from the spice market in Istanbul, Scottish tartans, Irish linens, African mud-cloth, Thai silks, and olive oils from Italy, Spain, and Greece, and tea, wine and liqueurs from everywhere.

It's all precious and personal, which is the point. High on the wall in my dining room is a saying, painted by hand: "This corner of the world smiles upon me above all others." I can't take credit for the phrase – I saw it carved into the face of a mantelpiece in a 19th-century Pennsylvania farmhouse-turned-inn, during a summer-stock tour in the 1980's with Bonnie Franklin. She, Shelley Fabares and I were there for cocktails. I remember how the presence of the man who built the house seemed palpable, his particular stamp and style was still present there, not least in the words glowing from the mantel above a roaring fire. And so a few years later, in an attempt to reclaim my space after a rather painful break-up, I had that thought emblazoned on a prominent wall. Now as then, it exemplifies how I feel about my environment.

When I see sparse, Zen-like, minimalist homes in books on interior design, I appreciate the simple grace, the tranquility that the lack of possessions suggests. It seems as if it would free your mind … but I'm not sure I could ever really live like that. In my photos and objects, I retain so much of the people and cultures that have moved and inspired me. Maybe my Wonder-Bread-and-Miracle-Whip upbringing has made me unusually fond of the exotic, primitive and unknown. But in my collection of items from around the world, I see proof positive that we all are one people.

My accountant Annette, a no-nonsense woman, does not always approve of my culture-hopping sprees of "retail therapy." So often after I've sent her bills to be paid, I have received E-mails from her with just four words: "What are you thinking?!"

But as I look around my home I see a large canvas of clouds that draws me into the eternal. I see a scroll of a Chinese Grandfather, arms raised, spinning a tale for his small grandson (and think of Gramp). There is an art piece of a medicine God from the Andes that blesses me … graceful birds my friend Roy carved that humble me by the time and love spent creating them … angels, Buddhas, crosses, paintings with faces that feel to me like spirit guides.

They perform for me every day. I always see new things that intrigue me, that move me when I am open to thinking about them and looking at them in different ways. I am constantly surprised and comforted and visually stimulated.

Mind you, if a friend were to come in and move an object from its place, it would be a matter of minutes before it was back in its home. And I want to see them. Collecting, for me, is a kind of nesting. It is a making yourself comfortable by gathering talismans that bring me comfort. It feels ritualistic.

As a child, I was so bounced around between so many people that I had no one, fixed vision of home. So when I moved to New York and it came time to create my world, it was essential to create a place of beauty, harmony and dependability where I had absolute control. I also realize, now, that because for so long I never considered myself a physically attractive person, designing my home became a way to feel attractive by extension. Home is the place where I can never be made to feel insignificant or invisible. I had a pillow embroidered that says *"Je me contente de ma peau"* – I am content in my skin. And at home, I truly am. I am less guarded, more engaged, engaging and accessible.

Often when I walk into a gallery and see something that really moves me, I have to have it. It's as if rather than my choosing it, it chooses me. It is that reversal that is so powerful.

I've always enjoyed the beauty of my home, but something happened after I was told, with the HIV-positive diagnosis, that my life might be cut short. I became exponentially more acquisitive – and, because soon after I began working on cruise ships that took me around the world, the variety and extent of what I could acquire increased dramatically. Shopping the planet became a race to fill my home with various expressions of lifestyles, cultures and heritages. Somehow in the affirmation that peoples from the Andes to Alaska, from India to Istanbul I realized that we are all truly one, it affirmed my connectedness with something greater than myself.

Colliding cultures en route to infinity. It expresses a passion and a certain kind of courage. So, like my mother always said: "A dollar down, and a dollar when they catch me!"

Me as Raoul

THE PHANTOM YEARS

"No more talk of darkness, forget those wide-eyed fears ... "
– "All I Ask of You," *The Phantom of the Opera,* Andrew Lloyd Webber

When my then-agent, Jim Wilhelm, called to tell me I had an audition for *The Phantom of the Opera,* I said, "You've got to be kidding. A year and a half ago, they told me I was too old to play the romantic lead."

"You're still too old to play Raoul. This is to cover the Phantom and play a Fop. You're perfect!"

"Leading men don't do Fops."

"They do if they get paid."

"When and where?"

The audition was at the Majestic Theater where *Phantom* had been running for some time. My heart sank when I approached the stage door. I uttered a little prayer that Hal Prince, a director with whom I longed to work, would not recognize me from my audition for Raoul the year before. Just thinking about it left me cringing. Since then I had lost weight, was blonder, and had a look of health and rest that I didn't have the year before while I had been caring for Granny. I had looked old, heavy and heavy-hearted – anything but "leading-manly."

As I walked backstage, I was greeted by Stage Manager Fred Hanson and Musical Supervisor Kristen Blodgett, who had been the musical director in a production of *Tom Jones* I'd done some years before. She told me that indeed Mr. Prince was in the front of the house. I joined a group of pacing, warming up actors who appeared to be as nervous as I was. But then projection loves company.

After what felt like an eternity, my name was called and I walked out onto the stage to sing "Music of the Night" on the spot where Michael Crawford had become a legend for singing that very same song. It appeared my prayer was answered. Gratefully, either Hal must not have remembered me from the year before or kind enough not to mention it, because after I sang all of the Phantom's material, he asked me to do "All I Ask of You," Raoul's romantic duet with the heroine, Christine.

I went home feeling good about what I had done and the next day got a call from Jim saying that I'd been offered the Broadway company, Fop and all. Two days later, when I was out working a hideous part-time job which I needed at the time to make ends meet, I called in for my messages. To my surprise, there was a very excited Jim telling me to go home, pack a bag for myself, and head for LaGuardia. Hal Prince had recommended me to Garth Drabinsky for his new production of *Phantom* in Toronto – to play Raoul!

It was late on a Friday afternoon, I had no cash, no prospect of getting any (before ATM's) and my flight left in two hours. Quickly I made my excuses at work, where rather than wishing me well they said, "You're fired!" I jumped on a subway, went home, threw my leading man drag into a bag, borrowed $50 from my neighbor Jack, and hailed a cab. A taxi ride at rush hour is never a soothing experience and I remember this one as particularly exhilarating, or maybe it was just that I was in high gear.

The good news was I made the plane. The bad news was by the time we got to Toronto, the weather was so bad that, after circling many times, we returned to LaGuardia and sat on the runway for two hours. Finally, the prisoners were released. We were allowed to stretch in the lounge area at the gate. As the blizzard in Toronto subsided, we re-boarded, sat for another eternity at the gate and, finally, landed on what looked to me to be a glacial ice field.

I had never been to Canada and had childhood romantic images of the Royal Mounted Police. What confronted me was more like Nanook of the North. After fighting with immigration over the purpose of my visit, I left the terminal to discover the car that had been waiting for me had long since left. At that time of the night (not to mention the blizzard raging) there was not a rental car, taxi, limousine, bus, or train to be found. Finally, I threw myself in front of a private car and begged them to take me into town.

At 5 a.m. when at last I arrived at the Four Seasons in Yorkville (Toronto's answer to Beverly Hills), I trudged wearily to my room, hoping to get at least a nap before my audition for Garth at 10 a.m. I ordered some hot chocolate to speed me to sleep; room service brought an elaborate tray, I crawled in between fine linen sheets, picked up the pot and poured... Nothing! The pot was empty. I just laughed and laughed and, I must admit, as I finally dozed off, it occurred to me that I probably was not meant to play Raoul, now or ever!

The morning started out much like the night before. I was exhausted, puffy-eyed, and cranky. An overly cheerful car service driver picked me up. We slid more than drove to Roy Thomson Hall to meet with Garth; his first in command, Edgar Dobie; and Lisa and Bud Pierce, the Canadian Casting Agents. Garth was late so we began without him. I sang all of the material, certain that I had lost my shot at the role. Garth entered in a flurry, settled down with the others, and I was asked to sing again. I repeated all of the Phantom's material, all of Raoul's material, and read the scenes between Raoul and Christine.

By this time I was so tired, punchy and annoyed that I didn't really have anything to lose. I picked up Lisa, with whom I was reading the scenes, and dramatically carried her across the room. This act of bravado was uncharacteristic for me in an audition situation where I'm usually intent on being perfect, or at least cautious. They were so startled that I think it went a long way toward getting me the job. They all had a brief conference, after which Garth advanced on me, much like a bear on his prey. In what I was to learn later was a typical growl, he said, "Okay, kid. We want you to do this. Tell your agent to go easy on these negotiations." Being exhausted and having a back up, I told him I had been offered the Broadway company that week and it was really a matter of money. He growled once more and was gone.

I made my way back to New York and it wasn't long before I knew I was in an exquisite dilemma – I'd been offered both the Broadway and the Toronto companies within a week of each other. Unbelievable.

Until then, I'd been broke, desperate and deeply tired from taking care of Granny and completely discouraged about the state of affairs in the world of theater. I had felt minutes away from chucking it all and either going back to school or finding a mindless job somewhere, anywhere, that would give my life some semblance of normalcy and regularity.

The choice, then, was an easy one. I was burned out in New York. I wanted to get away from the apartment where I'd cared for Granny, the scene of her last days. Plus, I could make twice the money in Canada, and because this new production would be starring Colm Wilkinson – who originated the role of Jean Valjean in *Les Miserables* – it was likely we would do a cast recording. Going to Toronto solved so many dilemmas in one fell swoop. At last, I had the break I needed.

I was invited to lunch at Sardi's by Edgar Dobie to meet my leading lady, Rebecca Caine. She was quiet, smart, self-effacing and exquisitely beautiful. After a rather awkward lunch with attorneys and producers, she took me by the hand to the Majestic Theater to meet Colm who was there already in rehearsal.

The weeks flew by as I made my plans to leave New York for what I thought would be six months to a year. Little did I know it would turn into five. But it was all a blur of logistics and preparation. I made another trip to look for an apartment. I found the perfect place to make a home and made my first friend that day. Marilyn Fields, the real estate agent who showed me all over town, is an outrageously enthusiastic character...my first Jewish mother. Her generosity of spirit and vivacious energy reminded me just a little of Granny. She took me everywhere and showed me everything and introduced me to everyone. Across the years, Marilyn's mother filled my refrigerator with good, homemade food. Marilyn would hate the characterization as a Jewish Mother because she was neither old enough to be mine, nor did she have children. But she took me under her wing and I was grateful as she smothered me with affection, information and introduced me to seemingly everyone in Toronto.

I made other friends as well. One was Tina VanderHeyden. Tina was the Associate Producer on *Phantom* and also functioned as our company manager in the beginning of the run. She has a cool demeanor and exudes a quietly confident charm that immediately puts all at ease. No problem was too big or too small on my behalf. I actually developed a tremendous crush on her whole family. She had the two most beautiful children, and her husband John immediately made me laugh as if we'd been old friends for years.

The day before we began rehearsals, I had a party and invited my new friends, the cast, and the production team. Everyone came, even Garth. I welcomed them to my home, which looked as if I'd been there for years, having already brought up a vanload of personal effects (as I've said, I don't travel light). I worked like a demon to get everything ready, but it was worth it. I had been warned there was a feeling of resentment at my being the only American imported to do a principal role, which could have been played by a Canadian.

I thought (and rightly so, as it turned out) that getting everyone together in a social atmosphere would help us warm up to each other. I don't remember what I served that day, but I do remember the presentation was bountiful and, at the end, it was all gone. Actors love free food. Rebecca, my leading lady, broke a glass and spilled red wine all over the carpet. I took it as a good omen, much to her relief and my therapist's amazement.

Rehearsals were held in a small local theater. *Phantom* had been running in other cities long enough that the production team knew what formula worked for them. Garth had assembled an extraordinary cast and crew. And, as is typical of all his productions, this *Phantom* would be bigger and better than ever! And he was right.

The first days of rehearsal are always scary for me. I found my terror matched by Rebecca's and so we held on to each other for support. Garth, mistaking our clinging for chemistry, boasted of his brilliant casting. In truth, as rehearsals wore on we came to see that, indeed, we were a perfect stage couple and our chemistry would delight audiences. Our friendship and connection immediately brought depth and warmth to the production.

Rebecca presented delicious contradictions. She was bright, articulate, gorgeous, gifted, graceful, insecure, self-deprecating, and marvelously neurotic. We made a great pair of conspirators. It was never an effort to make love to Rebecca on stage. I immediately became her "stage husband." She did her off-stage "wifery" with Tim Richards, who also became a great friend.

The most terrifying moment in rehearsals came for me when it was time to do "the jump." There is a moment in the show where the Phantom takes Christine down to his lair. Raoul follows them, descends into the bowels of the Paris Opera House, and leaps from a bridge into what appears to be the Paris sewers. The reality of this glamorous moment is that I had to leap 20 feet through a hole in the stage about the size of a casket onto a stunt bag. They brought in a stunt man to show me the safest way to fall. In a private moment, he confided that he wouldn't do this stunt eight times a week. Great. But he showed me the best way to land without (hopefully) hurting myself. To tell the truth, I could hardly hear him. I was busy trying to absorb the shock of finding out this stunt frightened a pro. To make it worse, the first time I tried it was in front of Garth and the entire macho crew. Inside I was screaming. Outside I was Raoul.

The day we moved into the Pantages Theatre was very exciting. The theater had long since been broken up into a multiplex movie house, and had just undergone a $19-million renovation to bring it back to the original glory of its vaudeville days. Garth spared no expense, bringing in craftspeople from all over the world, and the result was dazzling. But no more dazzling than the opulent sets, costumes, wigs, and props that would produce the visual splendor of Paris at the mid-19th century. I was completely overwhelmed and a more than a little awed.

The fog and smoke machines … the 194 trap doors all connected to hydraulic lifts … the candelabras moving in and out and up and down … stairways larger than some buildings, moving on rollers … thousands of yards of fabric dropping from above … jeweled gowns that weighed more than the women who wore them … hundred of wigs hand-tied for the actors wearing them, and pounds of make-up … cameras and video screens under, over, and on the sides of the stage … the orchestra, which is an entire world unto itself … dressers running in every direction … the corps de ballet warming up in every nook and cranny, and vocal exercises echoing from all corners … mechanics, electricians, carpenters, the fly crew, photographers, press people, dignitaries, corporate sponsors, political VIPs, local and international celebrities. This was opening night backstage.

I was both exhilarated and terrified. I had received telegrams, calls, and well wishes from all over the United States and Canada. My friends were genuinely thrilled for me. Rebecca and I kept running back and forth between our dressing rooms, both of which were filled with enough flowers to satisfy the funeral requirements of a sultan. We both realized with giddy alarm that this opening was a very big deal.

And if we hadn't known that on our own, Garth poked his head in the door to say, "This is the most important night of your lives. Don't fuck it up!" I replied with Robert Browning's quote, "*A man's reach should exceed his grasp, or what's a heaven for?*" I don't think he got it.

Not only was this opening to be a jewel in the crown of Garth Drabinsky, it was a "cause celeb" for Toronto. Both the opening of *Phantom* and the reopening of the Pantages would be the subject of books and documentaries – and we were right in the middle of it all. Alone I my dressing room, wearing pink sponge rollers to give my hair the body God had not, I began to make the transition from Byron to Raoul. It suddenly struck me that I was doing what I had always wanted to do. I was a leading man in a major production where all the stops were pulled out. This was a spectacular moment. And I was ready for the curtain to go up.

As it turned out, I, along with the other cast members, had to wait for the curtain to rise that night until the National Anthem of each of the attending dignitaries' countries was played. We stood through "Oh Canada," "The Star Spangled Banner" and "God Save the Queen." Then the moment arrived.

The performance was thrilling, the audience overwhelmingly receptive, and the ovations and curtain calls were the stuff of dreams. Backstage, it occurred to me that I had suddenly become a bit of a celebrity – and even more wonderfully, was being taken into the hearts of the good citizens of Toronto. My pal, Bonnie Franklin had come up to be my date for the evening. She pushed her way through the throng outside my dressing room and showered me with praise. I must say I had no trouble accepting the acknowledgment I had for so many years longed and worked for. I loved every minute.

Bonnie and me at an Opening Night Party

   With Bonnie on my arm, we went to the opening night party, the spectacle of which rivaled that of the stage production. All of the streets around the Pantages were blocked off. There were so many Rolls Royces, limousines, and Daimlers that we could barely make our way to the car, which we shared with Lisa Pierce, the Canadian casting agent for the production and a delightful new friend. We arrived at Casa Loma, an outrageous architectural landmark and tourist attraction, built by an eccentric at the turn of the century to provide proper lodgings for Queen Victoria. For the occasion, Garth had hired the Canadian Ballet Company to dance, leap, and twirl about the castle as the guests arrived. There were also extras draped about the premises wearing period costumes. We passed through a walkway of trees created entirely of long-stemmed, red roses beneath a hologram of the Phantom's mask spinning in the air above the castle turrets.

Inside was a montage of rich food, fine wine, and dancers lit by thousands of candles. I met the Prime Minister of Canada, all the provincial dignitaries and representatives of the Queen, the American delegation, Karen Kain (Canada's prima ballerina), Andrew Lloyd Weber, and a long list of celebrities. One very cordial young gentleman was quite effusive. Just as I was about to introduce myself and ask his name, Bonnie grabbed my arm and whispered, "Don't!" It was Prince Edward of England. How was I to know? In America, princes were only in fairy tales. There were two or three parties after this and though they were a little less spectacular, Bonnie and I continued to have a delicious time.

At the end of the night, I dropped Bonnie off at her hotel and went home. As I drifted off to sleep, I thought about how wonderful it had been to share the occasion with such a close friend. And then I thought how even more wonderful it might have been not to be going home to an empty bed.

Someone once said that living in Toronto is like living in New York, only run by the Swiss. I fell quite easily into this new life; after 13 years shuttling back and forth between Manhattan and Los Angeles, I was thrilled at the clean and polite environs of Toronto.

I spotted Mark in the press room of a luncheon where we'd both been invited to sit at the head table. I was a token American added since Jack Valenti, president of the Screen Actors Guild, was speaking. Mark was involved in the film industry as well and on a board that was active in this meeting of The Empire Club.

Mark had a twinkle in his eyes and I could hardly take mine off of him. We spoke briefly and I wondered if I'd ever see him again. Was I imagining it or was there some spark there?

We lived in the same neighborhood and a couple of days later I found a note under my door asking if I'd like to go for a walk, have dinner or see a movie. I waited a long time before I called – about two minutes. We began a friendship that was exhilarating and, at first, disappointing: Mark was involved in a relationship of five years. I made my peace with it, met his partner, and we all became friends. In the meantime I was dating other people, but couldn't get Mark out of my head

Ultimately, he broke off his long-time relationship. He assured me that I was not the reason, only the catalyst. We turned a fast corner into romance. Our time together was challenging for both of us: In his former relationship, his partner worked in his firm, so Mark was the boss, at home and at work. They were together 24 hours a day, seven days a week.

Then there I was, an actor of all things, with a totally different schedule and style, and no one had ever been my boss. Mark would get up at dawn to go to the gym before work and when he'd be getting home and wanting to wind down after a long day, I'd be gearing up for the theater. I had two shows on Saturday and a matinee on Sunday. I'm sure it was a huge adjustment for him and he was lonely.

And we both were in tremendous periods of personal and professional transition. There was great love between us, but much disagreement as we faced the uncertainties all newly formed couples do. We had moved in together and gave it our best shot. But we were both stubborn and willful and despite our attempts to work things out. But I never seemed to be 'quite right' or 'good enough ...'

It was in the early days of the AIDS epidemic and neither one of us had been tested. I had long feared that I was positive and decided that if there was ever going to be a good time to find out, this was it. I was in a relationship, well employed and on a good road. The test results showed that my fears were well-founded: I was positive. Mark, though, was negative. Unconsciously, I think, Mark began to pull away from me. I don't know whether my diagnosis played a part or not. But shortly thereafter Mark and I became friends with another couple, Craig and Mack.

I'll never forget the day when I called Mark on his cell phone during the intermission of a matinee. It was unlike him not to be at work, and when he told me he was out for a drive in the country with Craig. I knew. Don't misunderstand. Mark and I broke up because we had problems of our own. But it was an amazing karmic lesson that there was someone else who was immediately a catalyst for our break-up, just as I had been for Mark's break-up previously.

Months went by. I went into therapy both to deal with my health status and to heal my heart. I decided the only relationship I was up to was a dog. My friend Donna Gliddon, a talented artist in hair and wig design, had two beautiful golden retrievers. Through her encouragement and help, I located an older dog that needed a home. Shelbi was perfect. We bonded well and she went everywhere with me. She slept under my dressing table at the theater, went to the gym, to many social occasions, and even to the market. Which brings me to Raymond.

An autumn day in Toronto, where I had lived for almost two years, I was driving in my brand new Jeep out doing errands, stereo blaring my favorite soundtrack, "Somewhere in Time." In an expansive gesture, I decided to call Garth to thank him. He responded with a characteristic growl. Life was good. I turned into the parking lot of my favorite market.

I was at the produce section of Mr. Grocer when I saw his amazing smile beaming from the checkout counter. I turned to see where he was looking and low and behold, it was at me! Trying to appear nonchalant, I went back to squeezing oranges which were by this time almost to the state of pulp. But when I turned around, he was gone. Disappointed and feeling stupid for not having acted on my impulse to speak to him, I proceeded to the bakery section, and there he was. He'd paid his bill, put down his bags and come back in. We spoke for a few minutes and he asked me to call him. In my usual and subtle way, I waited until I was in the car and left him a message. We had dinner that night.

It was quite a romance. I had recently released my solo CD and the *Phantom* CD had gone platinum twice (on its way to five times). So life was good. Raymond and I continued to see each other as various friends and family would visit. Just at the peak of my success and happiness both professionally and personally, I had no way of knowing just how abruptly things would change.

My departure from *Phantom* was less than auspicious. Garth wanted me to play a small role in his new production of *Showboat,* also being directed by Hal Prince, and understudy the leading role of Gaylord Ravenal. Although he assured me in the next production I would play the lead, I asked him if he would put it in writing. He feigned shock that his word was not good enough. I told him I'd learned a long time ago, "If it's not good enough to put into writing, it's not good enough." (Thank you, Granny).

It was time for my contract renewal for *Phantom* and, after five years, he was essentially blackmailing me. If I didn't take the *Showboat* job, there would be no place for me in *Phantom.* I thanked him for five wonderful years and left his office. Although he swore he'd never hire me again, a few months later I found myself in Vancouver once again playing Raoul, and also in Honolulu later that year.

Both in Vancouver and Honolulu, Raymond was able to join me for extended periods of time to travel with me occasionally as I did my concerts. And although our relationship was "largely undefined," to use his words, we saw each other (almost) exclusively for about a year. But when it became evident that it was time for me to return to New York, he couldn't make that move – and my career was there. So I returned to begin again, once more. Alone.

I couldn't help but wonder if my professional life would ever match that which I'd already experienced in Toronto. And although in many ways it has, it doesn't really matter. Because once a man has been part of something great, no matter how brief, that greatness stays with him.

HOME FOR THE HOLIDAYS

"Ah, yes. Family. The first, final, essential masterpiece."

– Linda Ellerbee

Home for the holidays? I didn't think so.

Holidays with my family have not, as an adult, been an option. Self-preservation, on my part. Partly because of the memories of the drama than inevitably surrounded them as a child. Partly because of the continuing drama that leaves me physically ill, emotionally exhausted and just plain old angry at the sheer waste of time and energy spent on rehashing the past and nurturing new hurts.

I grew up in a world of secrets, intrigue, partial truths, abuse and emotional blackmail contrasted sharply by grandparents who extravagantly indulged me to make up for the reality that was my life. Inevitably the holidays brought to a head all the demons that had not yet escaped through the course of the year.

There were the usual 'family reverting to childhood' roles and reliving unfulfilled dreams of what might have been. In our home – or homes, depending on which set of parents, step-parents or grandparents with whom we found ourselves – it was a time of excess, as we tried to make up for (or worked hard not to acknowledge) the reality of our situation and the dramas unfolding each year. Always different. Always dramatic. Always hurtful. Always present.

And so it went. Mounds of gifts from the adults to the kids to make up for the hurts and uncertain relationships of the year gone by – but along with the gifts came volatile dinners as relatives took the chance to act out on those we were supposed to love. Over time, I didn't know whether to look forward to the holidays or dread them.

Mostly, I remember being in the car trying to hit all the bases. We would always find ourselves rushing from place to place, always late, never spending enough time anywhere to satisfy our hosts or ourselves. I don't ever remember a Thanksgiving or Christmas of just being. It was always my job to be the best little boy to everyone. Everywhere. On the other hand, Joan, Sharon and I made out like bandits at all the stops. Many years later (after Dad and Jean were married) there were, at last, four peaceful holidays in their (our) home.

Church was always a part. I loved the music. And yet the whole manger thing never really made sense to me. I didn't understand what a virgin was or how the wise men got there in time. I couldn't decipher where Santa fit in either. But I knew enough not to ask. Children were to be seen and not heard and I would do anything not to incur the wrath of the players in our tribe.

Somewhere along the line in my adult years, after several peaceful Christmases and Thanksgivings in my own home, I made an attempt to go back one more time to Christmas in California to see if it was as if I remembered, or if time had colored my memories.

Christmas Day. I remember taking a nap to ease the migraine and nausea I felt. When I woke up, I looked across the long expanse of my father's home at a group that I realized didn't really know me anymore. They were no longer a part of my day-to-day world. And although we (they) were having a nice time, I felt like a stranger in a strange land. I did not return for the holidays for eighteen years.

In the fall of 2003, I went out to be with my oldest sister, Joanie, who was in the last stages of cancer. It was the week before Thanksgiving. Having just returned from a medical procedure of my own that left me feeling a little fragile, I arrived to find her dreadfully sick after two sessions of chemotherapy. I wanted to run. But I wanted Joan more.

Joan was staying in her daughter and son-in-law's home, Michelle and Mike. Michelle and her husband Mike were doing everything they could to keep family life going and take care of Joan, but it was tearing them (especially Michelle) apart. Sharon, my other sister, and Joan had gone through decades alternating between loving and supporting each other, and not speaking – and now, when Sharon wanted to accompany me on my visit and 'be there' for Joan, Joan wanted nothing of the sort. Into this already-seething cauldron of stress, my dad threw his contribution: He had received my friends' 50th-birthday letter about raising money to help me repair the medication side-effects, considered their actions 'well-intended invasion of privacy" – and asked to know why I had not kept him abreast of my complicated medical situation myself.

Mind you, in 20 years of my dealing with HIV-related issues, Dad had rarely inquired. So I began to bring him up to speed – and watched him sink lower and lower in his chair, confirming my longtime presumption that he's far happier not knowing. I know my dad loves me. But my world of New York, theater, friends, HIV and all it entails is, I think, mystifying and overwhelming to him.

My life in NYC was peaceful, though, compared to that family-gathering ala Peyton Place. So though my relatives urged me to stay a few more days to spend Thanksgiving, I made my excuses and escaped. Much as I love my family, it seemed as if we loved each other much better from a distance. Face-to-face, for me, it's almost impossible to be faithful to everyone's particular needs. As I thought about holidays gone by, a flood of memories washed over me. I do not have the luxury of a selective memory.

It wasn't all bad. I remember many childhood years when, the day after Thanksgiving we could get out my mother's crèche, beautiful Bavarian porcelain figures, while Mother sang along with Peggy Lee and Nat King Cole. I remember the year that Poppy (my ex-step-grandmother's second husband) glued a new $100 bill between two pieces of wood and told us our job to open it so that the money wasn't destroyed. I remember when the Santa myth began to slip – as I realized the shoeprints in the ashes around the fireplace always looked like Dad's oxfords had made them, and that Santa's handwriting looked somehow familiar….

One of those years, Dad gave me an electric train, and I was over the moon. I left his home to spend the rest of Christmas Day with Mother, Granny and Gramp. Granny and Gramp gave me a drum set which thrilled me and annoyed my mother. I guess I didn't respond as enthusiastically to her gift as I did to the drums and especially the train. Later that day, I found my new train set in the deep end of Granny's pool. Granny quietly drained the pool and we dried it off. It never really worked again, but I still have it, packed away.

Fast forward. Though I had fled from Thanksgiving and declined to join the family for Christmas, early in the new year I returned to visit Joan once more. She was back in her own home and receiving hospice care. Joan had always lived her life on her own terms and resolved to die that way as well. During those days, masked with morphine and tears, we had sweet times and talks together. On one, most precious afternoon, Joan, Sharon and I cuddled up on the bed holding hands, telling stories, laughing, crying and simply being together. Family. Nothing else mattered. Again I learned, you can love someone completely, without complete understanding.

Joan made her peace and let go. The rest of us struggled to comprehend that she really was gone. And I decided then that I would, no matter what, spend the next Christmas in California. I told myself it was because I wanted to be supportive of Dad and Jean. But in retrospect, I think it was because I needed to re-affirm where I had come from. My roots. My family. My connection.

I'm sure it meant more to me than anyone – and as usual, there were some uncertainties between some of us who've lived widely divergent lives for 30 years. But our bonds transcend all differences, all time and all logic. These people are my heart. They are my home.

Ah, yes. Family. The first, final, essential masterpiece.

Egypt at last!

TRAVELS WITH UNCLE MAME

*"Open a new window, open a new door. Travel a new
highway that's never been tried before ..."*

– "Open a New Window," *MAME*, Jerry Herman

*D*uring my run in the *Mame* revival, just before the curtain dropped every night at the Gershwin Theater, I would watch Angela Lansbury walk a small boy up the stairs promising to show him "things he never dreamed existed ..." Little did I know I would become "Uncle Mame" to many of my friends and relatives, when employment on the cruise lines allowed me to bring them along on many of my exotic travels. Going to sea shortly after the HIV diagnosis, when I thought my life was drawing to a close, I was determined to celebrate every adventure I could. And so I did.

It all began like this: I was teaching in one of the conservatory programs at NYU and not having much fun, or making enough money. I'd just gone through a rather painful breakup, so escape began to sound very attractive. Coincidence? Perhaps. But I heard somewhere that "coincidence is God's way of remaining anonymous."

What I did not know, when I first got the opportunity to perform on a particularly well-known cruise line, was that it was considered the top of the line for the big ships. Far from the Love Boat, it's more like a floating Ritz Carlton in its fine services and luxurious accommodations and appointments. For performing for cruise guests, I was paid in cash plus expenses, I could take someone along as my guest for free – and it was very little work compared to the rigors of theater. As opposed to eight shows a week during my stage career, as a cruise a headliner, I performed twice in 12 days. I had a first-class cabin with all the privileges that went with it. So when the opportunity to go to Africa presented itself, I decided to get over my pride and have an adventure.

There was another element as well. Although I felt well, the lab reports suggested a darker truth: The virus was creeping up on me. I remember thinking "You better go see the world now; God only knows how much time you have left." My doctor advised against it, saying world travel would present so many health risks to which I would be particularly vulnerable with a compromised immune system. But I decided that I was not going to make my decisions based on fear.

I promised not to do anything stupid and to take all possible precautions (not to mention a suitcase filled with medication, supplements and an arsenal of 'what if' preparations}. Going to the ships was a choice that also did not thrill my agent and probably stopped the momentum of my career dead in its tracks. But I resolved to make a life choice as opposed to a career choice. And so I left.

The first cruise was from Mombasa to Cape Town. My next door neighbors, Jack and Linda Vartoogian are renowned photographers who specialize in world music and dance. I called Jack to see if they, by chance, knew anyone in Mombasa. Amazingly, they did and put me in touch with a man called Chuni Shaw. Chuni was an importer there and invited me to fly in early and spend a few days at his home.

I flew into Nairobi and took a beautiful train ride across the cliffs along the sea to Mombasa. There at the train station stood a little man who looked rather like Gandhi. Chuni's parents were from India but he had lived in Africa for most of his life. There, he created a world and business that was quite remarkable. With two or three stores he had his own little empire. He lived in a pavilion, open-air style home that was overrun with men in sari-style skirts. I'd never seen such a happy household until I realized they all chewed a particular leaf that looks like spinach and acts like an amphetamine. No wonder they were so happy. They were most gracious and were willing to see to my every need.

I was not naïve. I had traveled before. Not wanting to overstep my bounds with my host or subject myself to other unknown possibilities, I accepted his generous guest accommodations and exotic (if mysterious) food. We had sumptuous meals of local fish and vegetables I'd never seen, grilled in spices I couldn't identify even under the bright moon. Bats flew high above the palms that arched over his compound in the balmy evening air. The stars looked like Disney gone mad.

At dawn I set out for my first adventure in that far off and exotic world, having no idea what was ahead. Because he was who he was in his community, Chuni had arranged a wonderful four-day luxury safari at a nominal "locals" price. I spent two nights in the bush in a tent outfitted with everything from sterling candlesticks and fine china to my favorite wine and the most delicious food imaginable. We began in Tsavo, a national park in Kenya and spent the days with sweeping views from Kilimanjaro across the plains to watering holes with herds of elephants. There were water buffalo, warthogs, zebras, giraffe, gazelles, antelope. We saw just about everything … but lions.

We spent the days traveling in open jeeps over roads so bumpy and deeply rutted that at the end of every sojourn, I felt as if my body had been put through a blender. But the sights we saw, from the six-foot-high anthills to the Maasai village, were new worlds for me. This kind of travel is the luxury of the wealthy and the envy of millions of Americans – and there I was in the midst of it all.

The first time I encountered rural people with goods for sale, I had no idea that bargaining was expected. What was so much money to them seemed so little by American standards. Eventually my guide took me aside and explained that the beautifully-beaded necklace and armband I'd just bought from a Maasai warrior (who looked to be about seven feet tall) cost about double the price I should have paid. I still didn't believe him and went on.

The Maasai people are astonishing: tall, lean with flawless skin, high cheekbones, flashing eyes and regal carriage. In their brilliant red robes, they performed a ritual tribal dance in which they would jump, seemingly without effort or preparation, and almost suspend in mid-air. If I had not seen it with my own eyes, I would not have believed such a thing was possible. It defied everything I knew about gravity and certainly made me feel like a lead-footed klutz. I've been told they drink blood mixed with milk. Perhaps that accounts for their beauty and athletic prowess. I'll stick with Dr. Pepper.

After two days out in the open, we arrived mid-afternoon at the Salt Lick Lodge. We'd seen many carcasses on the road; my guide explained that it was the time of year when the lions were teaching their young to hunt and kill. I decided not to go for a walk. The lodge itself was simple, clean and handsomely crafted. I expected Meryl Streep to come around the corner any moment saying, "I had a farm in Africa …"

I went to the front desk to check in and behind it stood a giant of a man who looked as if he'd been carved from the most beautiful ebony. Smiling eyes invited me to sign the guest register. This was quite possibly the most striking creature I'd ever seen, and I was not alone in this judgment. Over cocktails later that day, the other guests, male and female, were commenting on his grace, style and beauty. His name was Gibbons and he was affectionately known around the compound as King. Small wonder. Besides his looks and demeanor, he had been educated at Oxford and each syllable was as exquisitely parsed as the King James Bible.

Gibbons grabbed my heavy bags as if they were groceries, and led me from the main pavilion across a series of suspension bridges going from one lodge unit to another. These dwellings were round, with thatched roofs about two stories above the ground. When we arrived at #7, we entered a room that a designer from The Bombay Company would imitate, poorly. Wide-planked, highly-polished hardwood floors gleamed in the light the instant Gibbons opened the shuttered windows. Outside, a herd of antelope grazed in front of a rugged vista of rock and tall grasses stretching for miles before its gradual ascent to the hills. The room had a safari-style desk, a magnificent Victorian armoire and a king-sized bed tented by mosquito netting hung from the roof. The ceiling fans were like the ones the church ladies used on Sunday mornings only bigger, made of straw about two feet square, cooling the room as they gently swayed back and forth on a series of pulleys. Black & Decker, take a lesson.

I took my journal out to the deck overlooking the watering hole and salt lick, which was in fact an enormous chunk of salt next to a natural watering hole where animals had been coming for centuries. On these acres, some very smart person had created this lodge where we mere mortals could have a close up view of what nature had created. There was also an underground tunnel leading from the lodge to the edge of the watering hole, rather like a World War One army bunker with a glass roof. Here, if your timing was right, you could view, through the camouflaged ceiling, the animals as they came to drink and rest.

High trees arched over the deck like a cathedral of green. A couple of zebras and several enormous birds brightened the landscape as if they'd been placed there by some very clever stage manager. Writing in my journal, I was suddenly aware that it was totally quiet, and the animals had disappeared. In a few minutes, the reason became clear: two lioness came into view, with several cubs. They were so graceful, and the cubs so playful, wrestling, tumbling, growling and licking. Soon, the enormous male appeared and, after sniffing around a bit, settled in on the sand, paws crossed, looking like a father just home from work waiting for his dinner to be served.

I can't tell you how long I sat and watched them that afternoon. I can tell you I was so moved that, at one point, I became aware that I was hardly breathing. These proud and dangerous creatures were about one hundred feet away and I was mesmerized. It wasn't until it started to rain that I finally left and went back to my tree-house to shower and dress for dinner.

The formal meal was a strange yet wonderful contrast to the rugged environment. The dining room of the main pavilion had cathedral ceilings supported by enormous tree trunks notched together and polished till they gleamed. Candlelight, beautiful music, a roaring fire; champagne and the symphony of rain playing all around you – what a scene! On tables set with starched linen tablecloths and sterling flatware, we dined on local game and a variety of salads and unfamiliar vegetables and roots. I do remember the most delicious hot pudding drowning in some liqueur. It didn't matter what it was. After one bite, no one cared.

When at last I could hold my head up no more, I dashed through the rain over the bridge to my hut and collapsed with the intensity of such a day. My dreams were filled that night with fantasies in which, like Clark Gable, I was the hero of adventures to rival the best MGM epic.

About 3 a.m. I heard what I thought was, at first, a couple moaning with pleasure from the next hut over. Great – just what a solitary traveler wants to hear. The next sound was a roar, more like a freight train coming through the hut. It didn't register at first; then I realized it was the lions!

I threw on clothes and raced (bed hair and all) back across the suspension bridge, dove into the tunnel and into the tiny, now-crowded bunker where many guests were already jockeying for the best spot to see the lions watering after a night on the kill. I stayed until the last lion had left and realized that if I saw no more, the trip had already been worth it.

The following day I was back in Mombasa at Chuni's home, exhausted and happy, exhilarated and grateful. Gibbons still writes letters, in the language of a poet, from the intensity of his soul and the soul of Africa.

A taxi drove me to the place where the ship was docked. It was after dark and in that desolate and empty port, the ship looked like the Taj Mahal. I'd sailed before on other ships, but this loomed up into the night like something from another planet. What I was to learn is that life on board is indeed another world. Just not the world I'd anticipated.

And so, a three-year journey began that would take me to over one hundred countries.

Abidjan, Ivory Coast. My carefully blow-dried and sprayed hair had completely melted into my sunscreen and was now a wet beige ring around the neck on my favorite linen shirt. Even in the most far-off places, I at least begin the day with an attempt at being presentable (if not fashionable, in case the ghost of Granny was hovering). I am not particularly proud of this habit, nor do I recommend it to others. It just comes as naturally as brushing my teeth every morning. But on this day by 10 a.m., I already looked, felt and probably smelled like a drowned rat.

The market place was teeming with people from the ships in port as well as other multi-national shoppers. At one stall, I was doing some of the finest acting of my career, appearing not to be terribly interested in two masks I wanted desperately. Language barriers aside, in almost any flea market around the world you can haggle with a hand-held calculator for anything, from a grass skirt in Samoa to a troll alongside the fjords in the North Cape.

I was raised by relatives who not only did not know how to bargain but found it completely taste free. And yet, as a world traveler, I became shameless in employing any device necessary to carry off the treasures I found. In this case, the young lad with the widest smile I'd ever seen was not budging an inch. In a last ditch effort to have my way, I began to sing. At the top of my lungs. I created a mini-operetta as a device to convince him to sell me the objects in question for the price I wanted.

I have a big voice and, when properly motivated, am shameless. Perhaps being a preacher's kid had its advantages. I'm nothing if not full of hot air and the ability to pull in a crowd.

As this nice young man with the beautiful white teeth started squirming in his stall, I continued my playful bantering (or was it bullying?) with him. He went from astonishment to curiosity to embarrassment and finally to exasperated laughter. At last he gave in, if for no other reason than to get rid of me. It worked. Those masks now hang next to my desk. Thanks to a similar incident in Beijing, a "spirit house" went down in price from US$600 cash to $50 on my credit card, and now lives on my piano.

One outstanding benefit of performing on cruise ships was that the company would fly me in or out of a city whenever I chose. So, for instance, when I got off the ship in Bombay, I stayed in India for a month. When I flew to Beijing, I arrive two weeks early to explore Beijing and cruise the Yangtsea Sea. When I flew into South Africa, I arrived in time to drive for three weeks all over the countryside before my cruise; I spent two weeks in the Andes exploring before my trip around the Cape. What adventures I had.

By boat from Mumbai (the former Bombay), through a beautiful arch called The Gates of India, I visited Elephant Island, where intricate, ancient carvings of deities, some two stories high, have inhabited blackened caves where they were placed thousands of years ago. The shallowness of the waters dictates that you dock about a mile from shore and walk an unbelievably long plank to the beach. Along that endless path are women with enormous jugs and baskets on their heads offering everything from Coke to fresh fruit. At the bottom of the long, steep stair leading to the caves, there are men who offer to carry you up on a litter. On a hot day in India, whatever the price, it's a good offer. But what happens is, about half way up they put you down and if you refuse to double the fare, they leave you there stranded. It was not a problem for me because I could make it on my own. But it brought out my "Ugly American" contempt to see the bearers pull this scam on older or physically infirm people.

It was at The Gates of India that I saw perhaps the most heartbreaking sight of all my travels. There, on what looked to be a makeshift skateboard, was one of the most beautiful, angelic faces I'd ever seen on a young man. I'd guess he was in his early 20s, with a smile to light up the skies, eyelashes to rival Elizabeth Taylor's – and no arms or legs, just a torso wrapped in a loin cloth.

I was told that in India, people have children for different reasons. They might have one or two to support them in their old age, one to sacrifice to the military, one perhaps to go into religious service. Most importantly, they have large families to balance the religious populations – God forbid one sect outnumbers the other. And in this particular case, a family chose one child to be mutilated, to more pitifully beg for money. Shocking. Sad. Infuriating. Horrifying. And, I was told, far too common.

He's got the whole world in his hand, well at least the Taj Mahal.

After a few days in Mumbai, I traveled to Agra to see the Red Fort and Taj Mahal. I have seen incredible and diverse architectural feats all over the world, but until you have seen the Taj Mahal in person, all descriptions pale. I made sure I was there to watch the sunrise upon it. I saw it turn from midnight blue, to gray, to orange, to pink, to gold, to brilliant white. Astonishing. The irony is that it was built by a man to honor his beloved who died giving him so many children in such a short period of time.

Later in his life, the man's son imprisoned him nearby in another impressive architectural feat across a wide valley. I stood in the small chamber where this man was held prisoner for the latter part of his life. His only pleasure was to look out the window at the final resting place where he would one day join his wife. As he went nearly blind, one of his daughters took pity and embedded a diamond in the wall at just the right angle so that when he looked through, it magnified the vista sufficiently for him to continue his vigil till his death.

Flying in India is like flying nowhere else. To say that things do not run on time is an understatement. On one occasion when my flight had finally left, literally a day late, I was reading an on-board magazine story about Kajurajo, where the Kama Sutra Temples are located. I always thought of Kama Sutra as simply being different positions and techniques of sex. Having visited there, I now know differently.

I decided to go to Kajurajo to take in an arts festival – but there was ultimately a much greater learning experience in store. I toured several of the 78 temples. I learned that orgasm, that moment of absolute ecstasy and connection with another human being, is when many people believe you are the closest to being one with God. And I experienced serendipity, a word I've always liked - and one that came to life while I was there.

When I asked the hotel concierge for suggestions for my free afternoon in Kajurajo, he mentioned a young man who offered tours to the local game park, and asked if I would be interested. I said, "Sure, please have him call." About a half hour later, he showed up and appeared not old enough to drive. But he assured me that he was 18 and had been doing this for many years. Accompanied by his 15-year-old wife – to whom he'd been married for three years – we left in his open jeep.

After a couple of hours, we reached the game park. By this time, I think I'd swallowed my weight in dust. Because of the time of day and the time of year, we saw no animals. At last he turned to me and said, "Mister, I think we see nothing today. But my wife comes from a small village not far from here where no tourists ever go. Would you like to see it?" Would I? A little dust never killed anyone.

We drove another half hour or so. I saw dozens of people walking for miles and miles: In order to work, most of them get up long before dawn to walk to their jobs and it is well after dark when they are home again. Just as I was beginning to worry about being kidnapped, we turned into a thicket so dense I didn't think we'd make it through. At last we entered a clearing: The village.

There were 20 or 30 low huts, made of something like adobe. They were open on all sides with fireplaces in the middle that burned cow dung for fuel. And they smelled like what they were: home to both the villagers and their livestock. Cows, goats, chickens, dogs, cats, monkeys and humans all living together as one.

When I stepped out of the jeep, it must have looked to them like I'd landed from outer space. They had never seen a blonde, or anyone of my height. They had never seen a camera and when the flash went off the adults scattered; the children stayed, intrigued. Their eyes had been painted with black all around to ward off evil spirits, and despite the filth by our standards, they were beautiful of face. Their bodies were clearly malnourished, distended bellies and thin little legs; some bore the evidence of lice and ringworm. As they crowded around, it suddenly occurred to me that I was making myself vulnerable to God knows what maladies and remembered my doctor's stern warnings. But it was too late: I was there, and I didn't want to leave.

The women were draped in bright colors, as are all the women in India, rich and poor. They asked for nothing, with one exception. One of the mothers asked (through my guide) if I had any soap. The next day, I bought all the soap, shampoo and candy I could find, to send to this village. Unlike so many of the aggressive people in the rest of the cities, neither the children nor the adults were asking for anything. They just wanted to be close, to touch, to see.

I spent several hours being shown around and showed off. They offered me food and tea which I felt obligated to accept, no matter how it tasted to me or what it might deny them that day. I sang to them. The scores of *Oklahoma* and *Camelot* were not in their repertoire, but they wanted more. They smiled. I cried.

Late that evening, as I was comfortably ensconced in my bed, I realized that I might as well be on another planet. I had planned to come back and shower, go to dinner and see some local dancing. But as on many of my days in India, I was so much on visual and emotional overload, I could barely move.

I had always known that, to a degree, that most of life is perception. Perspective. How you hold things. But suddenly I was aware that there is indeed an entirely different reality, not just within one nation, but within our own neighborhoods and sometimes even in our own homes. We all have different experiences of the same people and situations.

I visited the magnificent ruins of former splendor in Fatapursikri. I rode an elephant up the side of a cliff to enter the palace of a Maharaja in Jaipur, where once there had been a true floating garden in the middle of the palace. The elephants lined up like taxis at a taxi stand. I learned of the hundreds of deities in the various sects and practices of the religions there. I visited Sarnoth where Lord Buddha gave his first teaching and took a leaf home from the Bodhi tree. Having read Gandhi's biography, it was also important to me to visit the grave of this man that had so changed the world in such total humility.

And the adventures continued. By the time I boarded the cruise ship in Beijing, I'd already spent three weeks in China. My friend Julie joined me for this trip and through a friend of hers in the film industry, we were connected with a lovely woman at the University for the Studies of Foreign Language. In turn, she put us in touch with a young student who (as a trade-off) served as our guide to the Great Wall, Forbidden City and Summer Palace. He was as eager to practice his English as we were to see the sights. He wanted many questions answered, mostly about the Beatles. We wanted to hear the Beijing Opera, see Chinese acrobats and eat our weight in Peking Duck.

When I boarded the ship a second time in Africa, I went in a month early and drove all over South Africa with a friend. We saw Swaziland and rode a microlight aircraft over Victoria Falls. I learned about Shaka Zulu in his village and delighted in the tribal dancing and music, so rich in its legends and traditions. I found myself on a sunset cruise on the Zambezi River alongside crocodiles longer than my car; hippos surfaced and submerged in the water as elephants poked their heads through tall grasses.

Before going around the Horn in South America I traveled with my friend Nancy to Iguazu Falls, which makes Niagara Falls look like a trickle. We climbed to Machu Picchu and saw the glorious Andes. At Lake Titicaca we arrived at the small village on the shore where I'm sure the festival in progress was to herald our arrival. After a day of drinking the coca tea (to help adjust to the altitude) we took a boat to visit the floating islands of Lake Titicaca. Hundreds of years ago, the tribes in that region were at war with each other. Legend has it that one tribe took to their canoes, which were made of the weavings of thick grasses. They escaped the more powerful warriors by anchoring their canoes together in the middle of the lake. As the years went by, the canoes grew both because the silt collected and the tribal council decided to add to the weaving till they actually formed small settlements.

Miguel's Island was the first we visited. It was called that because the head guy is Miguel. The islands are literally like enormous floating doormats. If you stick an oar from their canoes through the 'floor' you can see that they are about four feet thick. On Miguel's Island, there are about five structures built for three families who live there.

They have never been off these islands. Ever. They grow corn, potatoes and other vegetables and live off these and the fish they catch. They sell the beautifully-embroidered textiles they weave to tourists who visit. Theirs is a very simple existence: No electricity, phones or connection with the outside world other than those who visit. They do everything in the water: eat, swim, fish. And, we were told, no one on these islands lives past 40.

We continued on through the Straits of Magellan, circling to celebrate Carnival in Rio, where, after I experienced the most insanely-wild, weeklong, citywide party, I went hang-gliding. I was uncertain about this particular adventure until I was told you are strapped to a Brazilian "pilot." Having seen the population on the beaches there, it took very little persuasion. At 6'3", I rarely feel dwarfed. But my pilot, Paulo, looked down at me – with turquoise eyes. In a thickly-accented voice that sounded like liquid gold, he said, "You must do everything I say and trust me. I have done this many, many times."

Hang Gliding in Rio

Okay, I'll say it again. I'm weak. Minutes later we ran in tandem off the side of Sugarloaf Mountain with Paulo strapped to a trapeze-type bar connected to the glider wings, and me strapped to him. The winds were good that day and we stayed afloat for about 30 minutes. At first we were over land, looking down on the village below; later we floated over the crystal-clear ocean, looking down at enormous stingrays and beautiful powder-white beaches. Attached to the edge of the glider wing was a camera, which Paulo controlled with a remote switch. The photos are thrilling as was the entire experience.

In Alaska I went dog sledding, ice rappelling, whale watching, fly fishing, white-water rafting, and walked on a glacier after flying above the ice fields.

I climbed a pyramid in Egypt (and got busted for it). I rode camels in Jordan on my way to Petra, and elephants in Bali and in India. I had breakfast with chimps at the Singapore Zoo. Somewhere there's a videotape of me while in Spain, singing "Granada" on the stage of the amphitheatre at the Alhambra in Granada. I parasailed in Mexico, and strolled the endless passages of the Kasbah in Casablanca. I kissed the blarney stone in Ireland, went hot-air ballooning in Provence, threw my coins in the Trevi Fountain in Rome and climbed the Rock of Gibraltar with the monkeys. I stood at the bottom of the world in Antarctica and marveled as the sun never really sets at the North Cape. I even went to the Falkland Islands. Three times. I'm not sure why.

These adventures are only a few drawn from the journals, photos and memories I have tucked away. But that's another book.

Life on board the luxury cruise ships was both wonderful and disconcerting. Although I had the status of a first class passenger, I was not one of the paying guests. Neither was I crew. The entertainment department was an entity unto itself. And so the challenge became not so much about your art, as how to achieve the best quality possible with a less-than-enthusiastic band and technical department. For them, getting us in and out felt rather like a shift change in a factory.

The response I received from the audiences was always gratifying, both at the curtain call and in the comments I personally received in the days following. But all the ship's performers were also rated formally. At the end of each cruise, guests fill out a ratings form that covers every aspect their time on board, from food to activities, personnel to entertainment. I regularly heard cruise line employees acknowledge that the ratings numbers were a poor way to measure artists' performance – and yet the home office lived by them, like the Bible. Ultimately, as an artist, my resentment at living under the ratings gun outweighed the pleasure of the work.

By the time I stopped cruising, I had truly seen, as my friend Frances Weaver said, "the fringes of the world." I have now been to almost every country where land touches water. But for that time, I had also completely taken myself out of the loop in New York, professionally and personally. No life between trips. And so I went home. But it was great while it was great. And even more than the travel, I made lifelong friends with both passengers and other guest entertainers and lecturers for which I will always be grateful. Not to mention the tchotchkes.

A tourist sees what he comes to see. A traveler sees what he sees. Having experienced the extraordinary diversity of all these cultures, I have come to know that I am both tourist and traveler. My journeys have only begun in heart, mind and spirit. And the souvenirs I brought home have much greater value than either their beauty or function. They make me feel more alive, somehow. Less arrogant and self-satisfied, more open and tolerant. These remembrances of things as wild as the lions in Africa remind me that life isn't always so tidy. That's part of the adventure.

Machu Pichu

Profiles

Bali

Bhutan

Shanghi

Sitka

Aphesis

Look closely at these photos. What's missing? Another person. Mostly, I saw the world alone.
But it was better to have taken the journey alone, than to never have taken it at all.

IF THERE'S AN ART DEALER IN HEAVEN

"You are my Sunshine, my only Sunshine.
You make me happy when skies are grey.
You'll never know Dear, how much I love you,
Please don't take my Sunshine away!"

– Jimmie Davis and Charles Mitchell

The walls of my sister Joan's home were covered floor to ceiling with oversized canvases and posters in bold, primary colors. She had a discerning, eclectic eye. Her house was an amazing collection that suggested joy, a passion for cooking, travel, antiques, adventure and most of all, a love of her family. Photos everywhere. Only the ceilings were bare. We once joked about building another hallway just to create more hanging space. She embodied the family's motto, "Less Is A Bore." But in all of her adult homes (I remember four), she created – generally on a budget – an inviting world of beauty in a style all her own.

In choosing a gift for Joan, the prevailing wisdom had always been: anything blue, anything nautical, or anything nude. She loved all things to do with the sea, from sailboats and exotic shells to lighthouses and mermaids. Much of her art had a theme of the idealized woman; and yet in most of her paintings, there was something obscured, some detail missing so as to deny you the entire story. I often wondered if it was that mystery that intrigued her.

Joan was one of the most beautiful women I've ever known, yet her self-image did not match. To the world, she showed an open, friendly personality; behind it, she was shy and uncertain. Although she had been married and delighted in her daughters and grandchildren, Joan was pretty much a loner. Yet on the day when we gathered to celebrate her life (not just mourn her death) the realization of how many lives she touched was overwhelming.

Much of the furniture had been removed to make room for the caterers and her precious companions Dusty and Princess (the most devoted and smelly dogs imaginable) were gone. But Joan's presence in the house was stronger than ever. Beautifully-framed photographs of her at every stage of her life were displayed as if in a gallery. Her extraordinary plants (ferns were as large as small cars) graced the Spanish-tiled patio. Joan had insisted on no memorial or funeral – just a party, casual and fun. She specifically asked that attendees wear jeans and Hawaiian shirts. Her sophisticated taste in art, music and literature belied a very simple style. Joan was more comfortable barefoot on the beach than anywhere – except perhaps Nordstrom's or the Laguna Art Festival.

My earliest memories of Joan – Joanie, in those days – were as my protector. At a time when our mother was unable to look after us, Joan took on the task. Our sister Sharon was only eighteen months younger than Joan, but it had taken another nine years for me to come along. So she was as much mother as sister to me in those years.

She did her best to shield me from the uncertainties – and sometimes, brutalities – that defined our home. Her first instinct in times of trouble was always to love, to protect, to help. And so Joan's lifelong role as caretaker and worrier was born at a very early age.

I always knew that I could call Joan first thing in the morning. Although I lived two time zones later than she, I'd still be struggling through coffee and *The New York Times* while early-riser Joan was well into her day and might well have washed the kitchen floor, polished silver or done a couple loads of laundry. She had an amazing work ethic at home or in the office. Her enthusiasm and energy was boundless. On one visit to New York she arrived on the "red eye" and while I wanted to go back to bed for a while (given the previous late night doing a show), she was eager to begin sightseeing immediately – at 5 a.m. And so we did.

I've heard it said that "death ends a life, but not a relationship." I prefer to think of it as Buddhists do: "Farewell and death are only different descriptions for a new beginning and life. All that you are leaving behind you will find again ... in different form and shape." I feel sure that not only will I see Joanie again; but that the best parts of her I carry in my heart.

When I was first diagnosed with HIV, Joan said: "Fine. You'll move home with me. I'll get an extra job so you won't have to work, and I'll take care of you." Typical.

Fifteen years ago, Joan sent me a needlepoint pillow that says "Expect a miracle." When she was diagnosed with cancer the first time, I sent it back to her. Later, when I was going through a rough patch, she sent it East to me once more. And when I learned she was sick again, I sent it back to her in San Diego. I saw it on one of her many bookcases, staring at me, on the day we gathered to celebrate her life. And though Joan's miracle may have been fulfilled in a better, more perfect place than I find myself, I'd rather have her back for just one more hug or to hear her on the phone, playfully asking across a continent: "I just made coffee, 'wanna come over?"

The "Expect a Miracle" pillow found its way back to me, thanks to Joan's daughters. It looks just right in my home – but sometimes, I wonder what her heavenly home looks like, now. I don't pretend to know about the realities of spirit beyond this world. But I like to picture Joan in a cozy room with a beautiful view of the sea, red wine in hand, deciding where to hang her latest treasure from some obscure, divine gallery.

"How strange it seems with so much gone of life land love, to still live on." – John Greenleaf Whittier

Joan Caroline Nease

CHAUTAUQUA

"You're a grand old flag, you're a high flying flag ... "

– "You're a Grand Old Flag," *George Washington, Jr.,* George M. Cohan

The 21st Century has not touched Chautauqua, which looks like a giant set for *The Music Man*: pure Americana. On the grounds are a series of beautifully restored Victorian homes with wrap-around verandahs complete with porch swings, rockers, hanging ferns, flower baskets – and the feel of more graceful, friendly days gone by. You almost can hear the echoes of horses delivering milk and groceries. And you actually can hear the voices of children singing out "Buy the morning paper, 50 cents" as they stroll through the narrow streets.

There are no vehicles allowed on the grounds, only pedestrian traffic and bicycles. There is an expansive square built around a huge green in the midst of winding streets filled with little jewels of houses ... all of them on a gentle slope that falls gently to Lake Chautauqua.

The conference center, originally built in the mid-19th Century as a Bible campground, is where the arts meet politics, philosophy and religion. What you cannot describe, until you have experienced it, is the remarkable spirit of the people who attend conferences there and, in many cases, have done so across the decades. There are generations of families that meet every year for one or more of the nine week-long seasons. During the annual celebration of "Old First Night," in the enormous amphitheatre, participants are asked to stand to signify how many years they have been attending. At the end of this exercise, one woman was left standing: She had been there every summer for 93 years.

One of my favorite moments was when they asked everyone to stand who had attended for every summer of their lives, and an elderly man stood proudly holding the hand of his great-grandson. It cut through the demographics of age and right to my heart. Young and old related to each other, not separated by schools, jobs, retirement homes, televisions, answering machines, computer screens, gated communities or other things that isolate us. The church services, opera, musicals, ballet, lectures, classes, discussions and recitals create an environment of abundant and diverse activity.

Having experienced Chautauqua the previous summer, I decided to take Dad and Jean for a week's adventure in 2000. The theme of the week I chose was "Developing a Healing Consciousness," which sounded as if it had been created with us in mind. I was hopeful that this place of inspiration might provide a time of healing and understanding of our family's differences and uncertainties.

I always exhale deeply as I drive across the George Washington Bridge leaving New York City. My breathing changes; I can feel my shoulders dropping and my pulse slowing as the tensions of the city melt away against the increasingly beautiful landscape of the rolling farmland and countryside. On this day, I was particularly exhilarated en route to Chautauqua. The previous summer I'd attended a writer's group there led by my friend Frances Weaver. As she'd told me, "No one leaves Chautauqua unchanged."

I picked up Dad and Jean at the Buffalo airport. We made our way out of town on a two-lane highway lit by a magnificent sunset overlooking Lake Erie. The summer green landscape contrasted dramatically to the desert terrain, where they live.

Almost immediately, Jean began a verbal campaign trying to encourage me in the notion that family was everything. She recited incidents from her experience as an administrator in a large retirement facility that had taught her "it's the family who counts, and in the end is there for you." As our drive and conversation continued, I realized what was driving her: a concern about my having created my own extended family in New York, while somewhat distancing myself from my relatives on the West coast.

I'd arranged for a beautiful little apartment right in the middle of the campus. From our second-story porch, we could overlook the enormous amphitheater where the larger events were held. From this vantage point we could hear the morning services: preachers, organists, readers and choirs. The roster that week included Neil Sedaka, Mary Chapin Carpenter, The Everly Brothers, *The Mikado*. There were recitals of piano, organ, marimba, and string quartets. The lectures ranged from music therapy and guided imagery to Hamilton Jordan (former chief of staff for Jimmy Carter) speaking about his three battles with cancer.

At Chautauqua, there are so many choices it is impossible to do it all. But we got a wide sampling of excellent programming. For me, the best part was just being together, sharing morning coffee, strolling through the narrow streets where it's traditional to display arrangements of gladiolas in every color and configuration. We spent time shopping (not Dad's favorite sport), eating too many ice cream cones and catching up on our busy and very different lives.

Throughout the week, our conversations kept coming back to the importance of family. Jean loves her siblings and was devoted to her parents. She and Dad have always longed for our blended family to be close, forgiving and supportive. It has not turned out that way. We have been separated by time, distance and too many hurts, some spoken and some never fully articulated. I have been the furthest away both geographically and philosophically.

It finally came to a head late one evening after a concert when I couldn't talk about it anymore. I excused myself and went to bed. I worried about having cut Jean off and hurting her feelings, knowing that her conversation was well intended. But I couldn't pretend to a familial trust. The next morning I tried to explain why I couldn't make a blanket statement that in an emergency or in a life threatening situation, I would turn to my family.

I remember as a little boy hearing my Aunt Ann say, "I love my family, but I couldn't live without my friends." As an adult, I have created a family of friends. I would do anything for them, and they have been there for me in ways I would never have dreamed possible. But with my family, time and again it has been made all too clear that my motives were suspect, that my sexuality was deviant, that my life in the theater was unstable – that whatever I did was not enough, not quite the right thing. I have never felt I inspire the kind of confidence, trust and respect from my family that I have in my friends and colleagues.

I was touched that Jean made such an effort to let me know that if I ever needed them, they would be there for me. When she noticed a Gay & Lesbian event and encouraged me to go, I was very moved by her efforts to be open about a subject that had for so long been hidden, ignored, fought over, hurt over.

I guess it's understandable given the level of denial and guilt we all practice to "make it through," the revisionist history we employ to find relief at any given moment. But I believe, ultimately, that resorting to these evasions leads to regret.

Ours is certainly not the only family with drama. It is my belief that by sharing our stories we will all realize that we are cut from the same cloth. We all have problems, failures, abuse, sadness, betrayal. But the good news is that with enough love and compassion, we can live through it together and, with luck, reach some degree of understanding and acceptance. It does not mean that we all like each other or always agree. It means we acknowledge and grow through the realities of our lives rather than pretending they never happened.

In the midst of the wonderful community of Chautauqua, generations, cultures, religions and political philosophies collide. In this place where diversity is celebrated and honored, Dad, Jean and I reached a greater and more realistic understanding and acceptance of each other. Perhaps it was the ice cream, morning coffee or just having the time to think together after years of distance. I returned them to the Buffalo airport with renewed hope.

Mom, Dad and Me

Sharon

TWINKLETOES AND MARTINIS

*"So we sit in a bar and talk till 2:00, 'bout life and love
as old friends do ... and tell each other what we've
been through ...how love is rare, life is strange, nothing
lasts ... people change."*
– Getting My Act Together – Gretchen Cryer & Nancy Ford

For my sister Sharon's 60th birthday, I gave her a pillow that says "I hope you dance" along with a gift certificate for dancing lessons. For years, Sharon has talked about wishing she knew how to dance. While traveling with me aboard ship, she would look wistfully at the couples on the dance floor. She even dragged me into one of the complimentary classes. One, I don't like it. And two, I don't do it well. I even titled a show I co-wrote *Leading Men Don't Dance* (the proof of which has been in the jobs I have NOT gotten across the years).

But despite our upbringing, Sharon has always wanted to dance. In our father's church, it was considered a sin. But Sharon and Joan would sneak off at family gatherings with our cousin Vic and "sin" away. She comes from a long line of sinners in that respect. Our mother danced in the Megland Kiddies with Judy Garland and Shirley Temple. She was a wonderful dancer, elegant and graceful. And Granny loved to dance so much she would, on her lunch break, head straight for the Coconut Grove at the Ambassador Hotel in downtown Los Angeles and spend her lunch hour gliding, twirling and having the time of her life.

Sharon's daughter Kim gave her an absolutely beautiful 60th birthday party, right on the ocean at sunset. It was a wonderful evening filled with laughter, toasts and a few tears. When our dad got up to give the final champagne toast, he bestowed upon her a new nickname: "Twinkletoes." And I intend to torture her with it for as long as we live – isn't that a baby brother's job?

Sharon and I did not really get to know each other until we were adults. Because of our age difference, she has more memories of me as a child than I do of her. As a matter of fact, although she says she loved me (and I *think* I believe her), until I came along to steal her thunder, she had been "the baby" and gotten the attention typically accorded to the youngest. So not only did I remove her from that coveted position, I was a boy, and had the nerve to be cute. It's a wonder we became friends at all.

Sharon always appeared serious and studious, especially after she got glasses. She practiced piano by the hour and it gave me great pleasure to jump out from behind the furniture and scare her. I think she still looks over her shoulder when she plays.

Sharon, however, persevered and became an accomplished musician and went off to San Jose State College when I was in one of my many grammar schools. From there she moved with her husband (also a pianist) to Washington and when he was awarded the prestigious Fulbright Scholarship, they moved to Germany to complete his studies.

By the time Sharon returned, I was a teenager and she pretty much a stranger to me. Across the years, a couple of husbands for her and a few relationships for me as well, we became friendly. But we had grown up with the same people in different decades and had very different experiences of them. So along with memories of childhood love, there was a natural (if not distrustful) questioning of each other.

It wasn't till Sharon came to visit me in New York that we began to understand each other. On her first visit, I took her breakfast in bed on a sterling tray with an orchid. I don't think she knew quite what to make of it. That evening, before we went to one of my favorite sushi palaces, I introduced her to martinis. On an empty stomach, she was pretty well in another world by the time we had ordered the appetizer dumplings; we never made it to the main course. A tall blonde woman with her head in miso soup is not a good look.

Later, while Granny was living with me in New York, Sharon came to visit. None of the family really understood Granny's choice in this situation: an 87-year-old woman, selling her home in Southern California to move in with her single, gay grandson in New York City. But Sharon had the hardest time of all. In describing Granny's move, she once said, "It's as if she died." No one could believe that she was actually getting better care and more stimulation in my home than she was living on her own or would be in a nursing home.

When Sharon arrived, I was polite – barely. I wanted both of them to have a nice visit, but intended to make myself as scarce as possible. Finally after a few days of icy formalities, Sharon demanded to know why I was so distant and angry. And I told her – on the corner of 57th Street and Fifth Avenue, at the top of my baritone lungs. After that, we were okay.

A few years later, Sharon came to visit me in Toronto a couple of times while I was *The Phantom of the Opera*. When I told her I was HIV-positive, it really brought us closer together and we began to be friends as well as brother and sister.

But it wasn't until our mother died that we really bonded. It was a dreadful time filled with emotional minefields. Mother had died without a will and her seemingly nice husband turned out to be anything but. Though the money was gone, everything in their home was our mother's before the marriage, and much of that from our grandparents and great-grandparents. At the Ed's death he left it to his ne'er-do-well sons. So Sharon and I petitioned the court to be the trustees of our mother's estate and over the next four years fought for two-thirds of what we could *prove* was hers before their marriage. Fortunately, we had lots of photos and Sharon had managed to get Mother's jewelry out of the house before Ed's death. Still, by the time we actually were able to take possession, the sons had already looted the house of what they wanted.

During this period of time, we disagreed on many things; but our common goal and willingness to work together brought us closer than we'd been before. Transforming Sharon's home with Mother's things was one big episode of "Queer Eye for the Straight Guy" as I became her personal decorating bully. And subsequently Sharon has seen me through several surgical procedures, taking care of me with a devotion that is quite astonishing. One of my friends said, "Sharon looks like Byron in a wig" … or was it "Like Byron without a beard"? I can't remember. With Joanie gone, I treasure her even more.

Sharon has been an educator her entire life, primarily in music. Now retired, and with her two daughters out creating their own worlds, Sharon is enjoying her first granddaughter and grandson … now teaching her family the tradition of "retail therapy." As she fox-trots her way into this new period of her life, I know the world will not be safe (or at least not any art gallery or shoe store) as long as she's around.

The one image I will always cherish is when we met in Tahiti. Sharon was joining me for a cruise and had already spent a week in Bora-Bora. This usually conservatively-dressed school teacher got off the plane wearing multi-colored tropical clothes, a wreath of flowers on her head, strands of shells around her neck, a coconut purse, woven baskets full of the treasures she found and a smile that lit up the already dazzling South Pacific sky.

As Stephen Sondheim says, *"With so little to be sure of in this world,"* I know that I can count on one thing. There is nothing we would not do for each other. Nothing. Here's to Twinkletoes, and martinis.

❖ ❖ ❖

HAPPINESS FOR AN IMPERFECT SERVANT

"... till my trophies at last I lay down ..."

– Traditional Hymn

My friend, the author Charles Barfoot, wrote a sermon entitled "An Imperfect Servant." He borrowed that phrase from Senator John McCain, as he described himself when endorsing his one-time political rival, George W. Bush, at the Republican National Convention in 2000. What an astonishing statement for a political leader. What a tremendous example for me.

Those words rang true and resonated deeply. They echoed family dictates of my childhood. They took on additional meaning as I struggled to build a career in a world where appearances are everything, but ultimately meant nothing if you could not deliver the goods – and even then, there were no guarantees. They shadowed me as I faced the ultimate test of looking at my mortality head on, taking stock of my achievements and failures. No one could be harder on me than me, even as I projected a sense of "Everything's fine!"

Charles quoted the Apostle Paul: "We do not lose heart. Even though our outer nature is wasting away, our inner nature is being renewed day by day." As I watched my body and face wasting, I finally had to really look at where I assigned value. The one thing I wanted more than anything was to make a difference to someone. And the way I knew best was through singing, speaking and telling my story. It's what I had to offer that no one else could.

And so I began to tell the reality of my story. First privately to my family and friends, then widening the circle to colleagues and, finally and very publicly, in the place I began: the church. Then came interviews, writing articles, doing benefits and finally this book. If indeed God's grace is sufficient for us, as Paul said, "I will boast all the more gladly of my weaknesses."

When I began, I thought it was a gamble. But I found such power in sharing the truth of my story. It has strengthened and sustained me. Combine that power of spirit with the miracles of the medical world, and the prayers and help of my friends and colleagues, and the only thing left was to figure out how to be happy in the midst. Truly happy. Learning to live with myself, rather than by myself.

Linda Ellerbee once told Maria Shriver, "Celebrate the struggle."

Celebrate the Struggle. Hmmm …

So, from my struggles, what have I learned? That if I ignore the past, if I re-invent history or simply deny it, if I do not keep moving forward and *choose* happiness and authenticity, then I will never stop fighting yesterday's battles. I will not be fully alive in this moment, able to embrace and be joyful with what I have. St. Thomas Aquinas tells us that "Joy is the noblest human act." I choose to be happy, as a way of life.

In the words of my father, *"Happiness is the faith in my capacity to overcome the inevitable difficulties of life and use them as tools to build a better world for myself and those I love."* It's about authenticity.

The biggest secrets are the ones I've kept from myself. I've learned that a lie of omission is still a lie, and that we are indeed, as sick as our secrets. As Martin Luther King said: *"There is a time when silence becomes betrayal."* Especially for me, in regard to my own thoughts and actions.

Happiness is the freedom to be authentic. It is the freedom of accepting responsibility for my own choices, and sharing the stories that collectively paint an accurate picture of who I am. Tricky stuff. Oscar Wilde said it best: *"The truth is never clear, and rarely simple."*

Early on I was led to believe that ours was the only family with drama so great that it must be hidden. What I've learned as an adult is that there are no families without drama, no human beings without secrets. To the degree that we deny that truth to ourselves and others – or even dare to think we're hiding it from God – we imperil our health and well-being, physically, emotionally and spiritually.

"Ol' Man River" – I remember when Gramp used to sing that song. I can see him at his piano in his smoking jacket, with his rich bass-baritone booming as he went off the lower end of the keyboard on the lyric " … or 'ya land in jail." Most of his life was spent with a cane or crutches and yet with all of his difficulties in life, I never heard him complain. Ever.

I've been thinking a lot about him lately. I look at my circumstances and see aspects I wish were otherwise – but I realize they will not change until I act, even if that means only shifting my consciousness into a place that resonates with happiness, peacefulness, gratitude. No matter my challenges, that 'Ol Man River keeps rolling; I can either go with the flow and enjoy the ride, or swim upstream.

Sometimes, I've realized, the path of least resistance is not such a bad one. Not that I give up: I'm just more careful about where I fight my battles and put my energy.

A few years ago when my niece Julie heard from her mother that I was writing this, she asked, "Why would you write a book about our family? Haven't we been hurt enough?" When my dad heard that I had signed with a literary agent, his first words were "I'm sure you won't say anything to embarrass your family." Both made me look at my motives. It is not my intention to embarrass or compromise those who populate my world, to hurt or betray. To the contrary. What I have discovered in reappraising my family history is that there were more acts of heroism, under the circumstances, than I'd ever realized.

To my niece's and dad's concerns about my telling my story, all I can say is: The strength is in the seeking and in the sharing, so that we all understand that we are not in this alone. We are bigger than our memories, or our feelings about them. We are bigger than our fears of the judgment of others. And we can choose, as my father once told me to, "replace judgment and blame with forgiveness."

On doctors' orders recently, I began a regimen of steroids, testosterone, sleeping pills and anti-depressants in an effort to feel better. What transpired over time was a spiral downward that almost resulted in suicide. A complicated combination of the chemical balance in my system and taxing life circumstances did exactly the opposite of that which I intended. I was so despondent, I'd even resurrected the stash of morphine and Seconal I'd kept in the early years for a peaceful "slipping away" when I thought there was no hope against the HIV/ AIDS. Now in retrospect, with the loving help of my friends, I can see the effects of depression can be powerful beyond our consciousness. And so, cold turkey, I went off everything but the most basic of my HIV meds. Within days, I felt myself again. I felt happy. I felt my life's possibilities. Hell, I simply felt. With therapy and determination, I press on, yet again seeking re-invention in the face of adversity.

In a stirring speech to the Republican National Convention in 1992, my friend Mary Fisher declared that true courage is not the absence of fear, but "rather the strength to act wisely when most we are afraid." I'd never had much experience with or empathy for people who were physically depressed, back when I had had no experience of it. Now I understand what a friend meant when she described it as like wearing an unshakeable suit of chain-mail.

My focus now is on shedding that armor and keeping it off. I have shifted my thinking and disciplined my actions to the end that there is nothing more important than my being happy every day. Some might say that sounds selfish. But when I wake up and focus on that which will make me happy, I am a better man not only for myself, but for everyone in my world, and in all I do.

I'm not talking about singing a chorus of "Da Queen of Denial." For instance, this morning, I got up to pay my bills. There was that file on my desk that I dread every month. I had put it off (as usual) for as long as possible. As I opened it up and looked at the pile of bills versus the balance of my account, I broke out into a cold sweat. So I closed the file until I could find a better thought about paying my bills. And I put on a favorite CD and listened to that great old song, "Count Your Blessings" whose lyrics include this line: *"When my bankroll is getting small, I think of when I had none at all … and I fall asleep counting my blessings."*

I looked around a beautiful home filled with the treasures that chronicle the journey of my life. I looked at the smiles in the faces of the photos of those I have loved and who have loved me so well. And through that act of will – that choice of joy, not despair – I remembered that I am bigger than the balance of my checkbook. I am bigger than my career. I am bigger than the virus I fight every day of my life. I am bigger than my past. I am bigger than my mistakes and fears.

I went back to my desk and suddenly the pile of bills was simply information. I didn't feel afraid or inadequate. I paid the ones I could, put the rest away and decided I'd find a way to make it happen when I can. I was able to be in the midst of the uncertainty and still be calm in my heart.

And so happiness has become truly enjoying the journey rather than pining for the destination. My life has been a vehicle of learning. I've grown in confidence that pain and disappointment cannot only be tolerated but, ultimately, be a blessing in disguise as an opportunity for growth. Peacefulness does not equate with ease. Peace is when you can be in the midst of chaos and still be calm deep inside. My tears do not determine my strength.

In theatrical rehearsals, we often employ improvisations to explore a character or situation. It is a journey of discovery as we do our work and probe into all the possibilities of a full-blown character. We discover that the roads we travel (on stage) are for the journey, not the destination. Each scene is important and informative – not just the final curtain. And most significantly, when we think we are fooling others, we are really only fooling ourselves. Audiences always know when you are "acting" as opposed to "being." As in life, authenticity is all.

And so I offer this to you. Our stories may vary in the details, but we all want and need basically the same things, as one of my favorite songwriters says: *"To be loved, to be happy, to have hope ... "* We have a legacy to leave if we choose, of tolerance and forgiveness. We can learn not just to listen, but to truly hear the stories of each others' lives. And we can gaze, with loving acceptance and appreciation, at the faces behind the masks.

A LOVE LETTER TO MY DAD

I have served a full life sentence as a prisoner of my past
As a victim of a victim of a victim
Seems my parents' parents' parents left traps
that held me fast
And they still catch me when I think I've licked 'em
Well, I have blamed them, I have fought them, but
I never understood
All they really did was did the best they could
Is there a way to rise above, if I look at them with love,
Though I look at them full honest in the face?
Can I make my peace at last, with the pieces of my past
And enfold them in forgiveness' embrace?...

Some call it wisdom, and some just call it grace
When we make our peace at last, with the
pieces of the past
And enfold them in forgiveness' embrace.

— "Forgiveness' Embrace," Stephen Schwartz

*S*easons. Seasons of life, of love and relationships.

Last summer my nephew was married. In the dozens of photos was one of me straightening my father's tie. It's a very sweet photo that I immediately had framed for him and for me. When Dad received his, his playful comment was, "Who is the old guy?"

We used to be the same height, and now I am several inches taller than he. As the son becomes the father and the father, the son …

A few months ago, if someone would have told me I'd be moving back to California where it all began, I would not have believed it possible. Yet summer is over, fall has fallen and the winter is just beginning to appear in life, as it does on the calendar.

Recently I sang a concert in southern California. After spending a few days there, I felt an enormous tug at my heart to be closer to my dad and stepmother. Dad is now at the end of his eighth decade and Jean, though a decade younger, is in equally uncertain territory in regard to health. Much of their lives these days are simply about survival and bouncing from one health scare to the next.

Knowing their circumstances, my first instinct was to swoop in and intervene, to try to fix everything – to make sure that all that could be done, was. But the truth is, I need to be there for me, perhaps, even more than for them. As I move through my own life's seasons, I do not want to have regrets.

In my larger-than-life family, I'm never sure which among us needs forgiveness and understanding the most. But increasingly in the past few years, I've heard my dad talk about his late father – about how he wishes he just could sit down and talk to him, ask him questions, seek understanding. I know how he feels, and am determined not to squander whatever time he and I might have left to be together.

My earliest memory of Dad was standing at his side as he greeted the congregation at the little church at the corner of 'C' and Lemon Streets in Ontario, California. I idolized him as he mesmerized the people in his congregation. But in his private moments I also cherished the man who knelt by his desk in prayer, and taught me to play catch; who pushed me on the swings at John Galvin Park, indulged me with chocolate malts at Foster's Freeze and snuck me into movies even though it was against the rules of his church; who taught me to drive (that was fun and a half), made me join the swim team and, even when I never won a race, cheered me on. I treasure him even more today, this man who still sings silly songs in the car and banters playfully (if shamelessly) with every waitress in his path.

In my home, there is a Chinese scroll that asks: *"How well did you live ... how well did you love ... how well did you learn to let go?"* Dad watched and let me go for the first time on my two-wheeler bike ... then as I left at age 17 to sing on the road for a year and yet again when I went off to college, and finally when I moved 3,000 miles to make my way in New York City and walk my own road to manhood. So much letting go. And as another of my favorite song lyrics says, *"The hardest part of love is letting go"* – especially when you are holding on with your heart.

Because of the physical distance between us for most of my adult life, it has been difficult for me to think of Dad as getting older. In the intimacy of our correspondence and in the laughter of our phone conversations, his voice is strong, his mind sharp, his humor intact, and his spirit indomitable. There is always a playfulness, a youthful energy, an optimism that sees him through.

St. Thomas Aquinas tells us that *"Joy is the noblest human act."* In that way, my father is a noble man – a man who, in the most difficult days of his life, has been heroic. He maneuvered through challenges with grace, strength, humor, style

... and as necessary, a touch of denial. I inherited that from him – along with my bald spot!

Like many fathers and sons, we have not always agreed. But Dad kept showing up as best he was able, no matter what reality I'd drag him into ... listening, advising, laughing, crying, bullying and loving. He speaks from his heart and tells his truth – a truth he believes will guide me in the ways of what he calls "intelligent love and loving intelligence."

I have a letter of his that I laminated and have kept on my dressing table for years. "Don't be afraid to be the best," it says. "Don't allow the detours of other people's choices to steer you away from the quietly confident, integrity-based decisions that strong men choose." He has not always understood or approved of the turns my life has taken. But it was he who taught me that we all have the power – the responsibility – to find our own true course.

As I look at my hands and face, and into my heart, it is clear I'm cut from this man's cloth. A loving and playful spirit is his greatest legacy to me. The man who pushed me on the swings, who taught me to drive, and who challenges my thinking still – this is the man I love most of all.

And so now I have returned to the West Coast for whatever time we have, to be together again. I hope – I believe – that in this time we can, indeed, hold each other in forgiveness' embrace.

EPILOGUE

Knowing my Dad will have read this, I ask myself, at the end of his life and nearing the end of mine: why is it so important to still be 'the best little boy in the world?' What is it about the cosmic parental tug that keeps us all bound to our parents?

Through this cathartic process, there has been some closure, as well as a look at where I might be going. Through the journey of seeking my father's approval, I make no apologies. Because it is this journey, the journey of loving, fearing, anger, re-loving and finally appreciating him, that was the catalyst to investigate who I am. Though telling my story was significant to me, it was often easier to dwell on a relationship outside of myself than to deal with the pain of self-hatred. The journey to re-love my Dad was my primer. The journey to love me, is my life.

The Course In Miracles says, that the perception of the Devil is not that of an external energy or demon. The Devil is really our own self-hatred that resides deep in our hearts and minds. I cannot think of a more frightening place for him to dwell.

This has been my story. You have had your own journey, and many of you have had it far worse than I. But I believe that having the courage to face the ones we love and fear the most is the Sherpa that will take us all to happiness.

Thank you for allowing me to share my story. The human experience is not so different for any of us. How we handle the details of our lives and where we arrive at the end, are individual paths. I hope in some way, my story might pave the way to emotional freedom. It is a journey that I am on – finally.

I still endeavor to live up to the commitments I've made to my family, hoping in the most honest part of my heart that it may buy me some love. But at every step, I find most gestures rejected. What they do not know is, at this very moment I write and juggle my health challenges, diminishing income while still living some semblance of a balanced life, I am working four days a week at a night-shift as well as two other part time jobs to keep up appearances and live up to the obligations I have made and want so desperately to keep.

Till recently, I've kept it a secret from almost everyone. I was embarrassed. I feared that every illusion I'd created or wanted to create would be destroyed. To be needy and vulnerable was failure to me. But in finding the courage to tell more people, I was greeted with overwhelming love and support, and most importantly laughter. I am learning that without truth there is no real friendship or love.

It's not been easy to teach this old dog new ways of living. But the more I'm able to let go of past precepts and deceptions, the faster I'm coming to know me. I am just beginning to feel the enormous relief of authentic friendships and the rewards that lay within.

As my book goes to press, I am excited and a bit fearful of the day that past acquaintances,lovers, friends, family and strangers see me. My journey has been one of exploration, but it is not an ending – just a small step toward light, which I perceive as happiness and freedom. No Pollyanna ending here. Not everyone in my family kisses and goes off into the sunset. Not all the wounds are healed. But I have begun an irreversible journey forward with commitment and enormous zest to un-peal this onion I call my life.

It has been said, that we teach others what we ourselves need to learn. I have been a student of some of the greatest writers of our time and hope my open door of thought allows others their own journey of exploration. I've tip-toed, I've edited much, even to this day. Is it wrong? What is most important has been to incorporate without compromising integrity. All of my life, I've chosen to pretend to be someone else, both on the stage and sometimes off.

My professional life has been documented by numerous posed photos. This tome is the true photograph. It is un-retouched or photo-shopped. Though I wanted to put in a last candid photo that would reflect who I am today, in going through the volumes of photographs, I realized that photo has yet to be taken.

While going through the volumes of photographs chronicling my life on and off stage, I realized that none truly captured how I feel about myself today. So I end this tome with a blank frame, knowing that soon I will be able to have an authentic photo.

Like an addict in a meeting, "My name is Byron Nease, and I stand naked before you."

- NO MASK -

❖ ❖ ❖

A photo yet to be taken … a work in progress